New Cloud GCSE REVISION NOTES FOR SIR ARTHUR CONAN DOYLE'S *THE SIGN OF FOUR* - Study guide (with AQA-style sample assessment questions and notes)

by Joe Broadfoot MA
All rights reserved

Copyright © Joe Broadfoot, 2017

The right of Joe Broadfoot to be identified as the author of this work has been asserted in accordance with Section 77 of the Copyright, Designs and Patents Act 1988

ISBN-13:
978-1548338923

ISBN-10:
1548338923

Brief Introduction

This book is aimed at GCSE students of English Literature who are studying Arthur Conan Doyle's *The Sign of Four*. The focus is on what examiners are looking for, especially since the changes to the curriculum in 2015, and here you will find each chapter covered in detail. I hope this will help you and be a valuable tool in your studies and revision.

Criteria for high marks

Make sure you use appropriate critical language (see glossary of literary terms at the back). You need your argument to be fluent, well-structured and coherent. Stay focused!

Analyse and explore the use of form, structure and the language. Explore how these aspects affect the meaning.

Make connections between texts and look at different interpretations. Explore their strengths and weaknesses. Don't forget to use supporting references to strengthen your argument.

Analyse and explore the context.

Best essay practice

There are so many way to write an essay. Many schools use **PEE** for paragraphs: point/evidence/explain. Others use **PETER**: point/evidence/technique/explain/reader; **PEEL**: point, example, explain, link; **PEEE**: point/evidence/explain/explore. Whichever method you use, make sure you mention the **writer's effects**. This generally is what most students forget to add. You must think of what the writer is trying to achieve by using a particular technique and what is actually achieved. Do not just spot techniques and note them. You may get some credit for using appropriate technology, but unless you can comment on the effect created on the reader and/or the writer's intention, you will miss out on most of the marks available.

Essay planning

In order to write a good essay it is necessary to plan. In fact, it is best to quite formulaic in an exam situation, as you won't have much time to get started. Therefore I will ask you to learn the following acronym: **DATMC (Definition, Application, Terminology, Main, Conclusion**. Some schools call it: **GSLMC (General, Specific, Link, Main, Conclusion)**, but it amounts to the same thing. The first three letters concern the introduction. (Of course, the alternative is to leave some blank lines and write your introduction after you have completed the main body of your essay, but it is probably not advisable for most students).

Let us first look at the following exam question, which is on poetry (of course, the same essay-planning principles apply to essays on novels and plays as well).

QUESTION: Explore how the poet conveys **feelings** in the poem.

STEP ONE: Identify the **keyword** in the question. (I have already done this, by highlighting it in **bold**). If you are following GSLMC, you now need to make a **general statement** about what feelings are. Alternatively, if you're following DATMC, simply **define** 'feelings'. For example, 'Feelings are emotion states or reactions or vague, irrationals ideas and beliefs'.

STEP TWO: If you are following GSLMC, you now need to make a **specific statement** linking feelings (or whatever else you've defined) to how they appear in the poem. Alternatively, if you're following DATMC, simply define which 'feelings' **apply** in this poem. For example, 'The feelings love, fear and guilt appear in this poem, and are expressed by the speaker in varying degrees.'

STEP THREE: If you are following GSLMC, you now need to make a **link statement** identifying the methods used to convey the feelings (or whatever else you've defined) in the poem. Alternatively, if you're following DATMC, simply define which **techniques** are used to convey 'feelings' in this poem. For example, 'The poet primarily uses alliteration to emphasise his heightened emotional state, while hyperbole and enjambment also help to convey the sense that the speaker is descending into a state of madness.

STEP FOUR: Whether you are following GSLMC or DATMC, the next stage is more or less the same. The main part of the essay involves writing around **six paragraphs**, using whichever variation of PEEE you prefer. In my example, I will use **Point, Evidence, Exploration, Effect** on the listener.

To make your essay even stronger, try to use your quotations chronologically. It will be easier for the examiner to follow, which means you are more likely to achieve a higher grade. To be more specific, I recommend that you take and analyse two quotations from the beginning of the poem, two from the middle, and two at the end.

STEP FIVE: Using Carol Ann Duffy's poem, 'Stealing', here's an example of how you could word one of your six paragraphs: **(POINT)** 'Near the beginning of the poem, the speaker's determination is expressed.' **(EVIDENCE)** 'This is achieved through the words: 'Better off dead than giving in'. **(EXPLORATION)**. The use of 'dead' emphasizes how far the speaker is prepared to go in pursuit of what he wants, although there is a sense that he is exaggerating (hyperbole). **(EFFECT)** The listener senses that the speaker may be immature given how prone he is to exaggerate his own bravery.

STEP SIX: After writing five or more paragraphs like the one above, it will be time to write a **conclusion**. In order to do that, it is necessary to sum up your previous points and evaluate them. This is not the time to introduce additional quotations. Here is an example of what I mean: 'To conclude, the poet clearly conveys the speaker's anger. Although the listener will be reluctant to completely sympathise with a thief, there is a sense that the speaker is suffering mentally, which makes him an interesting and partially a sympathetic character. By using a dramatic monologue form, the poet effectively conveys the speaker's mental anguish, which makes it easier to more deeply understand what first appears to be inexplicable acts of violence.

Other tips

Make your studies active!

Don't just sit there reading! Never forget to annotate, annotate and annotate!

All page references refer to the 2014 reprinted paperback edition of *The Sign of Four* published by Penguin English Library, London (ISBN: 978-0-141-39548-7).

The Sign of Four

AQA (New specification starting in 2015)

If you're studying for an AQA qualification in English Literature, there's a good chance your teachers will choose this text to study. There are good reasons for that: it's moralistic in that the text encourages us to think about right and wrong.

The Sign of Four is one of the texts listed on Paper 1, which needs to be completed in 1 hours 45 minutes. As well as knowing a nineteenth-century text from back-to-front, students will also be expected to know a Shakespearean play in full. More about that later.

Bear in mind, that you also need to be prepared for Paper 2, which consists of answering essay questions on a modern text, and on two poems categorised as 'Unseen Poetry' and two poems from the AQA anthology.

AQA have given students a choice of 12 set texts for the Modern Texts section of the exam paper. There are 6 plays: JB Priestley's *An Inspector Calls*, Willy Russell's *Blood Brothers*, Alan Bennett's *The History Boys*, Dennis Kelly's *DNA*, Simon Stephens's script of *The Curious Incident of the Dog in the Night-Time*, and Shelagh Delaney's *A Taste of Honey*. Alternatively, students can chose to write on the following 6 novels: William Golding's *Lord of the Flies*, AQA's Anthology called *Telling Tales*, George Orwell's *Animal Farm*, Kazuo Ishiguro's *Never Let Me Go*, Meera Syal's *Anita and Me*, and Stephen Kelman's *Pigeon English*. Answering one essay question on one of the above is worth a total of 34 marks, which includes 4 for vocabulary, spelling, punctuation and grammar. In other words, this section is worth 21.25% of your total grade at GCSE.

AQA have produced a poetry anthology entitled *Poems, Past and Present*, which includes 30 poems. Rather than study all 30, students are to study one of the two clusters of 15, which concentrate on common themes. There are two themes which students can choose from: Love and relationships, or power and conflict. Within the chosen thematic cluster, students must study all 15 poems and be prepared to write on any of them. Answering this section is worth 18.75% of your total GCSE grade.

The 'unseen poetry' section is more demanding, in that students will not know what to expect. However, as long as they are prepared to comment and compare different poems in terms of their content, theme, structure and language, students should be ready for whatever the exam can throw at them. This section is worth 20% of your total grade at GCSE.

Paper 2 itself makes up 60% of your total grade or, in other words, 96 raw marks. Just under half of those marks, 44 to be exact (27.5% of 60%), can be gained from analysing how the writer uses language, form and structure to create effects. To get a high grade, it is necessary for students to use appropriate literary terms, like metaphors, similes and so on.

AO1 accounts for 36 marks of the total of 96 (22.5% of the 60% for Paper 2, to be exact). To score highly on AO1, students need to provide an informed personal response, using quotations to support their point of view.

AO3 is all about context and, like Paper 1, only 7.5% of the total mark is awarded for this knowledge (12 marks). Similarly, AO4 (which is about spelling, punctuation and grammar) only accounts for 2.5% of the total (4 marks).

Now let's go back to Paper 1. One of the difficulties with Paper 1 is the language. That can't be helped, bearing in mind that part A of the exam paper involves answering questions on Shakespeare, whereas part B is all about the 19th-century novel.

To further complicate things, the education system is in a state of flux: that means we have to be ready for constant change. Of course, everyone had got used to grades A,B and C meaning a pass. It was simple, it was straightforward and nearly everyone understood it. Please be prepared that from this day henceforward, the top grade will now be known as 9. A grade 4 will be a pass, and anything below that will be found and anything above it will be a pass. Hopefully, that's not too confusing for anyone!

Now onto the exam itself. As I said, Paper 1 consists of Shakespeare and the 19th-century novel. Like Paper 2, it is a written closed book exam (in other words you are not allowed to have the texts with you), which lasts one hour 45 minutes. You can score 64 marks, which amounts to 40% of your GCSE grade.

In section B, students will be expected to write in detail about an extract from the novel they have studied in class and then write about the novel as a whole. Just for the record, the choices of novel are the following: *The Strange Case of Dr Jekyll and Mr Hyde* by Robert Louis Stevenson, *A Christmas Carol* and *Great Expectations* by Charles Dickens, *Jane Eyre* by Charlotte Brontë, *Frankenstein* by Mary Shelley, *Pride and Prejudice* by Jane Austin, and *The Sign of Four* by Sir Arthur Conan Doyle.

Another important thing to consider is the fact that for section B of Paper 1, you will not be assessed on Assessment Objective 4 (AO4), which involves spelling, punctuation, grammar and vocabulary. This will be assessed on section A of Paper 1, which is about Shakespeare, and it will be worth 2.5% of your overall GCSE grade. In terms of raw marks, it is worth 4 out of 64. So for once, we need not concern ourselves with what is affectionately known as 'SPAG' too much on this part of Paper 1.

However, it is necessary to use the correct literary terminology wherever possible to make sure we maximise our marks on Assessment Objective2 (AO2). AO2 tests how well we can analyse language form and structure. Additionally, we are expected to state the effect the writer tried to create and how it impacts on the reader.

This brings me onto Assessment Objective 1 (AO1), which involves you writing a personal response to the text. It is important that you use quotations to backup your points of view. Like AO2, AO1 is worth 15% of your GCSE on Paper 1.

Assessment Objective 3 (AO3) is worth half of that, but nevertheless it is important to comment on context to make sure you get as much of the 7.5% up for grabs as you can.

So just to make myself clear, there are 30 marks available in section B for your answer on the 19th-century novel. Breaking it down even further, you will get 12 marks maximum the backing up your personal opinion with quotations, an additional 12 marks for analysing the writer's choice of words for effect (not forgetting to use appropriate terminology - more on that see the glossary at the back of this book), and six marks for discussing context.

As you can see, we've got a lot to get through so without further ado let's get on with the actual text itself and possible exam questions.

Previous exam questions

Notwithstanding the governmental changes to the grading system, it is still good practice to go over previous exam papers. To make sure that you meet AQA's learning objectives and get a high mark, make sure you go into the exam knowing something about the following:

- the plot
- the characters
- the theme
- selected quotations/details
- exam skills

CONTENTS

	INTRODUCTION	i
1	THE SCIENCE OF DEDUCTION	14
2	THE STATEMENT OF THE CASE	23
3	IN QUEST OF A SOLUTION	30
4	THE STORY OF THE BALD-HEADED MAN	34
5	THE TRAGEDY OF PONDICHERRY LODGE	40
6	SHERLOCK HOLMES GIVES A DEMONSTRATION	45
7	THE EPISODE OF THE BARREL	51
8	THE BAKER STREET IRREGULARS	57
9	A BREAK IN THE CHAIN	62
10	THE END OF THE ISLANDER	67
11	THE GREAT AGRA TREASURE	73
12	THE STRANGE STORY OF JONATHAN SMALL	77
13	AQA-STYLE ASSESSMENTS & NOTES	85
14	ESSAY-WRITING TIPS	115
15	GLOSSARY	120

narrator: Watson

1 THE SCIENCE OF DEDUCTION

from boredom when he has no case to solve.

Page-by-page analysis

Chapter One

Starts off with Holmes taking cocaine.

The opening chapter is entitled 'The Science of Deduction', so clearly the focus is going to be on private investigator Sherlock Holmes's method of detection (1). We may feel surprised that he can detect anything, given that he is 'scarred with innumerable puncture-marks', which suggests he's an inveterate drug-user (1).

His 'companion', Dr Watson, who also narrates, takes Holmes to task for his bad habit. We discover that Watson is afraid of confronting Holmes, but he does it anyway. However, the doctor needs 'Beaune' wine to fuel his courage, which suggests that he is a meek character generally (1).

wants him to stop.

Watson is also physically weak compared to Holmes, as 'the Afghan campaign' of 1878-80 has taken its toll on him (2). Consequently, he cannot 'throw any extra strain upon' his 'constitution' (2).

THE SIGN OF FOUR – STUDY GUIDE

[handwritten annotation: doesn't like romance, isn't romantic.]

We also discover that Watson is quite sentimental, at least in comparison to Holmes, who complains that his 'brochure' entitled 'A Study in Scarlet' is tinged 'with romanticism' (3). Holmes believes that the account should have been more about his 'unravelling' of 'curious analytical reasoning from effects to causes' (3). This suggests a huge ego and an obsession with science.

Holmes is very much a specialist and admits he has 'been guilty of several monographs', which indicate that he has been keeping busy writing in detail on subjects, such as: 'Upon the distinction between the Ashes of the Various Tobaccos' (4). Watson acknowledges his companion's 'genius for minutiae', which is an appropriate skill for a detective (5).

When he guesses that Watson has been to the post office, we discover how Holmes operates as a detective. Holmes reveals that if you 'eliminate all other factors' then 'the one that remains must be the truth' (6).

Nevertheless, Watson thinks he has stumped the detective, when he gives a watch as a test to see if Holmes can uncover anything about 'the character or habits of the late owner' (6).

Much to Watson's chagrin, Holmes reveals that the previous owner was 'a man of untidy habits', who final took 'to drink' (7). Watson is upset because the previous owner was his late brother. For all his brilliance, Holmes realises he has been callous, saying: 'I had forgotten how personal and painful a thing it might be to you' (7). Although Holmes is a genius, he seems to struggle when it comes to conducting himself in a social situation.

This time, Holmes has worked out the truth through the application of 'the balance of probability' (8). There follows a detailed explanation of how he has put together a whole story through scraps of evidence.

However, he needs a greater challenge than the tests provided by Watson to keep him away from drugs. His stagnation is represented through the pathetic fallacy of 'the yellow fog' (9). The 'dun-coloured houses' show how bored he feels by his current jobless predicament (9).

Luckily, an adventure seems set to begin as his landlady, Mrs Hudson announces the arrival of 'Miss Mary Morstan' (9). The reader wonders what this alliteratively-named probable femme fatale could possibly want with Sherlock Holmes.

Sir Arthur Conan Doyle: The Sign of Four (AQA-style sample question)

'Read the following extract [311 words] from Chapter 1 and then answer the question that follows.

In this extract, the reader is introduced to Holmes through the narration of Watson for the first time.

Starting with this extract, explore how Conan Doyle portrays Sherlock Holmes, as an eccentric character.
Write about:
- **how Conan Doyle uses language and techniques to portray Holmes as an eccentric in this extract**
- **how Conan Doyle portrays Holmes as an eccentric in the novel as a whole.**

[30 marks] → Strange / off person.

Sherlock Holmes took his bottle from the corner of the mantel-piece and his hypodermic syringe from its neat morocco case. With his long, white, nervous fingers he adjusted the delicate needle, and rolled back his left shirt-cuff. For some little time his eyes rested thoughtfully upon the sinewy forearm and wrist all dotted and scarred with innumerable puncture-marks. Finally he thrust the sharp point home, pressed down the tiny piston, and sank back into the velvet-lined arm-chair with a long sigh of satisfaction.

Three times a day for many months I had witnessed this performance, but custom had not reconciled my mind to it. On the contrary, from day to day I had become more irritable at the sight, and my conscience swelled nightly within me at the thought that I had lacked the courage to protest. Again and again I had registered a vow that I should deliver my soul upon the subject, but there was that in the cool, nonchalant air of my companion which made him the last man with whom one would care to take anything approaching to a liberty. His great powers, his masterly manner, and the experience which I had had of his many extraordinary qualities, all made me diffident and backward in crossing him.

Yet upon that afternoon, whether it was the Beaune which I had taken with my lunch, or the additional exasperation produced by the extreme deliberation of his manner, I suddenly felt that I could hold out no longer.

"Which is it to-day?" I asked,--"morphine or cocaine?"

He raised his eyes languidly from the old black-letter volume which he had opened. "It is cocaine," he said,--"a seven-percent solution. Would you care to try it?"

"No, indeed," I answered, brusquely. "My constitution has not got over the Afghan campaign yet. I cannot afford to throw any extra strain upon it."

LET'S ANNOTATE THE TEXT IN RESPONSE TO THE FIRST PART OF THE QUESTION:

Sherlock Holmes took his bottle from the corner of the mantel-piece and his **hypodermic syringe** from its **neat morocco** case. With his **long, white, nervous fingers** he adjusted the delicate needle, and rolled back his left shirt-cuff. For some little time his eyes rested thoughtfully upon the sinewy forearm and wrist all dotted and scarred with **innumerable puncture-marks**. Finally he thrust the sharp point home, pressed down the tiny piston, and sank back into the **velvet-lined arm-chair** with a **long sigh of satisfaction**.

Three times a day for many months I had witnessed this performance, but custom had not reconciled my mind to it. On the contrary, from day to day I had become more irritable at the sight, and my conscience swelled nightly within me at the thought that I had lacked the courage to protest. Again and again I had registered a vow that I should deliver my soul upon the subject, but there was that in the **cool, nonchalant air** of my companion which made him the **last man with whom one would care to take anything approaching to a liberty**. His great powers, his **masterly manner**, and the experience which I had

Comment [JB(]: implies that Holmes is used to dealing with chemicals and is, therefore, something of a scientist. In the

Comment [JB(]: Implies that Holmes pays attention to detail. It could indicate that details are more important than

Comment [JB(]: The word 'morocco' implies that he is more well-travelled than most, which could relate to eccentricity in

Comment [JB(]: Suggests an artist – also indicating an eccentric temperament

Comment [JB(]: SH is a man of strange habits

Comment [JB(]: Opulent surroundings mark SH out as rich, but strange (eccentric)

Comment [JB(]: Suggests that he is easily bored, which makes him different to others and therefore eccentric.

Comment [JB(]: SH is calmer than the average person, which again could imply eccentricity.

Comment [JB(]: Relatively unapproachable, which indicates that he is far from normal and is therefore a little

Comment [JB(]: Using alliteration, SH is portrayed as almost superhuman.

had of his many extraordinary qualities, all made me diffident and backward in crossing him.

> Comment [JB(]: Hyperbole emphasizes the above

Yet upon that afternoon, whether it was the Beaune which I had taken with my lunch, or the additional exasperation produced by the extreme deliberation of his manner, I suddenly felt that I could hold out no longer.

> Comment [JB(]: SH is a man of extremes, implying eccentricity

> Comment [JB(]: SH appears to be sleepy, as if divorced from the current situation, which clearly bores him. His intelligence could indicate eccentricity.

"Which is it to-day?" I asked,--"morphine or cocaine?"

> Comment [JB(]: SH is erudite, which links to superior intelligence and eccentricity. He is ready something 'old', which suggests that he is detached from the here and now.

He raised his eyes languidly from the old black-letter volume which he had opened. "It is cocaine," he said,--"a seven-percent solution. Would you care to try it?"

> Comment [JB(]: Cocaine was not illegal in 19th century, but it's use would be frowned and mark SH out as an eccentric

"No, indeed," I answered, brusquely. "My constitution has not got over the Afghan campaign yet. I cannot afford to throw any extra strain upon it."

> Comment [JB(]: Watson is contrasted to Holmes here, which emphasizes how far from the norm SH has travelled. Watson would be admired for having taken part in the Second Afghan War (1878-80) to keep the Empire intact.

Starting with this extract, explore how Conan Doyle portrays Sherlock Holmes, as an eccentric character.
Write about:
• how Conan Doyle uses language and techniques to portray Holmes as an eccentric in this extract

- how Conan Doyle portrays Holmes as an eccentric in the novel as a whole.
[30 marks]

Mark scheme

Indicative Content
Any valid interpretations should be rewarded. Answers could, however, include some of the following:

AO1 - Personal response
- Watson's perceptions of the strange eccentricities of his companion
- Holmes' apparent familiarity with cocaine use and how this defines his character
- Holmes' formidable, almost-superhuman qualities

AO2 - Writer's effect
- Use of language to describe Holmes: 'masterful' etc
- Use of contrast (with Watson) to portray Holmes as eccentric
- Particular words to suggest otherness: 'extreme', 'extraordinary' etc

AO3 - Context
- Apparent eccentricity suggested by habits etc (e.g. cocaine habit, although not illegal, would have been frowned upon)

- **Watson's involvement in the preservation of the Empire, contrasted with Holmes' more individualistic concerns**
- **Presentation of Holmes as expert detective**

2 THE STATEMENT OF THE CASE

Chapter Two

In the second chapter, entitled 'The Statement of the Case', we quickly discover that Miss Morstan is quite exotic: her 'turban' suggests that she has some connection with India. The narrator thinks she may be far from well off, as the 'simplicity about her costume' suggests 'limited means' (10).

While she oozes vulnerability and 'intense inward agitation' with her trembling lip and quivering hand, Holmes is the opposite. The contrast is emphasised by the description of 'his clear-cut, hawk-like features' (11). This shows he is like a predator, while she is prey in comparison.

We find out that the date is some time in late 1888 and that her father 'was an officer in an Indian regiment', which explains the turban (11). Her 'unfortunate father' has gone missing and she needs Holmes to investigate his inexplicable disappearance (11).

There are no obvious clues in his luggage, and the only friend he has in England is 'Major Sholto' (12). To add to the mystery, Miss Morstan tells Holmes that she has received a 'very large lustrous pearl' every year since, on the advice of her employer, she published her address in answer to an advertisement (12).

She also shows Holmes a letter which, amongst other things, tells her that she is 'a wronged woman' who 'shall have justice' (13). She is told to meet the letter-writer outside the Lyceum Theatre, but warned not to 'bring police' (13). However, she can 'bring two friends' (13). Luckily, Holmes and Watson are willing to take on the case and accompany her.

Although fascinated by the idea of solving the case, Holmes's lack of interest in people is evidenced by his comment that he 'did not observe' that Miss Morstan is 'attractive' (14). Watson is flabbergasted and calls Holmes 'an automaton - a calculating machine' (14). Once again, we see reason represented by Holmes opposed to Watson's 'emotional qualities' (14).

Holmes recommends that Watson read Winewood Reade's 'Martyrdom of Man', while he disappears for an hour (15). The intertextual reference suggests that Holmes is a social Darwinist, who believes in survival of the fittest rather than religion and sentimentality.

Watson, meanwhile, remains preoccupied with the 27-year-old Miss Morstan, whom he describes as at a 'sweet age' (15). He recognizes that ideas of a romance with her are 'mere will-o'-the-whisps of the imagination' (15). He describes his future as 'black', which shows a deep pessimism on his part.

Sir Arthur Conan Doyle: The Sign of Four (AQA-style sample question)

'Read the following extract [326 words] from Chapter 2 and then answer the question that follows.

In this extract, the reader is introduced to Miss Mary Morstan through the narration of Watson for the first time.

Starting with this extract, explore the representation of women.
Write about:
- **how Conan Doyle portrays Miss Marston**
- **how Conan Doyle portrays women in the novel as a whole.**

[30 marks]

Miss Morstan entered the room with a firm step and an outward composure of manner. She was a blonde young lady, small, dainty, well gloved, and dressed in the most perfect taste. There was, however, a plainness and simplicity about her costume which bore with it a suggestion of limited means. The dress was a sombre grayish beige, untrimmed and unbraided, and she wore a small turban of the same dull hue, relieved only by a suspicion of white feather in the side. Her face had neither regularity of feature nor beauty of complexion, but her expression was sweet and amiable, and her large blue eyes were singularly spiritual and sympathetic. In an experience of women which extends over many nations and three separate continents, I have never looked upon a face which gave a clearer promise of a refined and sensitive nature. I could not but observe that as she took the seat which Sherlock Holmes placed for her, her lip trembled, her hand quivered, and she showed every sign of intense inward agitation.

To my surprise, the young lady held up her gloved hand to detain me. "If your friend," she said, "would be good enough to stop, he might be of inestimable service to me."

I relapsed into my chair.

"Briefly," she continued, "the facts are these. My father was an officer in an Indian regiment who sent me home when I was quite a child. My mother was dead, and I had no relative in England. I was placed, however, in a comfortable boarding establishment at Edinburgh, and there I remained until I was seventeen years of age. In the year 1878 my father, who was senior captain of his regiment, obtained twelve months' leave and came home. [...] He came home with his heart full of hope, to find some peace, some comfort, and instead--" She put her hand to her throat, and a choking sob cut short the sentence.

THE SIGN OF FOUR – STUDY GUIDE

LET'S ANNOTATE THE TEXT IN RESPONSE TO THE FIRST PART OF THE QUESTION:

Sir Arthur Conan Doyle: The Sign of Four
(AQA-style sample question)
'Read the following extract [326 words] from Chapter 2 and then answer the question that follows.
In this extract, the reader is introduced to Miss Mary Morstan through the narration of Watson for the first time.
Starting with this extract, explore the representation of women.
Write about:
- how Conan Doyle portrays Miss Marston
- how Conan Doyle portrays women in the novel as a whole.
[30 marks]

Miss Morstan entered the room with a firm step and an outward composure of manner. She was a blonde young lady, small, dainty, well gloved, and dressed in the most perfect taste. There was, however, a plainness and simplicity about her costume which bore with it a suggestion of limited means. The dress was a sombre grayish beige, untrimmed and unbraided, and she wore a small turban of the same dull hue, relieved only by a suspicion of white feather in the side. Her face had neither regularity of feature nor beauty of complexion, but her expression was sweet and

Comment [JB(): Miss Morstan is portrayed as determined and unreliant on male strength, although later we realize she requires Holmes' assistance.

Comment [JB(): Miss Morstan is composed, which makes her more similar to Holmes than to a stereotypical Victorian heroine.

Comment [JB(): Hyperbolically described, makes her appear to be an angel, albeit one outside the home.

Comment [JB(): Her 'limited means' makes the reader sympathise with her. She is doing her best to look presentable.

Comment [JB(): There is nothing unpalatable about this thoroughly decent young woman.

Comment [JB(): Suggests that she is more worldly than most women, so atypical.

Comment [JB(): Implies delicacy and purity.

Comment [JB(): On a superficial level, she lacks beauty.

27

amiable, and her large blue eyes were singularly spiritual and sympathetic. In an experience of women which extends over many nations and three separate continents, I have never looked upon a face which gave a clearer promise of a refined and sensitive nature. I could not but observe that as she took the seat which Sherlock Holmes placed for her, her lip trembled, her hand quivered, and she showed every sign of intense inward agitation.

To my surprise, the young lady held up her gloved hand to detain me. "If your friend," she said, "would be good enough to stop, he might be of inestimable service to me."

I relapsed into my chair.

"Briefly," she continued, "the facts are these. My father was an officer in an Indian regiment who sent me home when I was quite a child. My mother was dead, and I had no relative in England. I was placed, however, in a comfortable boarding establishment at Edinburgh, and there I remained until I was seventeen years of age. In the year 1878 my father, who was senior captain of his regiment, obtained twelve months' leave and came home. [...] He came home with his heart full of hope, to find some peace, some comfort, and instead--" She put her hand to her throat, and a choking sob cut short the sentence.

AO1 - Personal response

Comments:

- amiable: Suggests she will be easy to control.
- singularly spiritual and sympathetic: Sibilance emphasizes how deep she is as a person.
- refined and sensitive nature: Victorians would generally consider these attributes as desirable as 'accomplishments' for young ladies.
- her lip trembled, her hand quivered: Typical portrayal of a weak and vulnerable Victorian woman.
- held up her gloved hand to detain me: She wields some power, despite seeming to be helpless.
- choking sob: Archetypal, weeping Victorian woman.

AO2 - Writer's effect
AO3 - Context

3 IN QUEST OF A SOLUTION

Chapter Three

The third chapter entitled 'In Quest of a Solution' begins at 5:30, when Holmes returns.

He seems to think it's an open and shut case, saying: 'there is no great mystery in this matter (16). Sometimes, the renowned detective suffers from over-confidence, and this is an example of it.

The narrative uses Watson's obtuseness or comparatively slow understanding to tease out more information from Holmes in a form that is digestible for the reader. Holmes explains that he thinks 'Sholto's heir knows something [...] and desires to make compensation' (16). Watson is an excellent foil for Holmes, as he questions his companion by saying: 'It is too much to suppose that her father is still alive' (17).

The tension increases as Holmes takes 'his revolver from his drawer' (17). This suggests that he is taking the matter seriously with the expectation of violence. Miss Morstan's 'pale' face adds to the impression that something dramatic is about to happen (17).

She shows Holmes a paper that was found in her father's desk, which reads: 'The sign of the four - Jonathan Small, Mahomet Singh, Abdullah Khan, Dost Akbar' (18). Holmes has to admit that he does 'not see how' it 'bears upon the matter', but nevertheless tells her to 'preserve it carefully' (18). Even if the characters do not know it, the reader is aware that it will be an important document as it echoes the title of the novel. The 'fog' that envelopes them emphasises the lack of clarity surrounding the case so is an example of pathetic fallacy (18).

At the meeting place, 'a small, dark, brisk man in the dress of a coachman' accosts them, checking that the police are not with them (19). He whistles to a ragged street urchin (street urchins were known as 'street Arabs' at that time), who takes them to a four-wheel vehicle. Then they are whisked away. It is all so mysterious, as the utmost secrecy appears to be expected.

It appears that Watson has maintained his relationship with Miss Marston, as he remarks that: 'To this day she declares that I told her one moving anecdote as to how a musket looked into my tent' (20). He is relating his scary 'adventures in Afghanistan', but the 'broad, silent water' of the Thames, which they cross, seems just as threatening (20).

They eventually reach 'a questionable and forbidding neighbourhood' in south London (20). Even the brick buildings are 'staring' (20).

The personification of the building makes it more intimidating. 'A Hindoo servant, clad in a yellow turban' opens the door (20). The colour yellow was often associated with decay and decadence. A 'high, piping voice from some inner room' is heard beckoning them in (20). The chapter ends on this cliffhanger as the reader wonders who the voice belongs to.

> **'Starting with this extract, explore how Conan Doyle uses setting to create a gothic atmosphere.**
> **Write about:**
> - **how Conan Doyle uses setting to create a gothic atmosphere in this extract**
> - **how Conan Doyle uses setting to create a gothic atmosphere in the novel as a whole.**
> **[30 marks]'**

It was a September evening, and not yet seven o'clock, but the day had been a dreary one, and a dense drizzly fog lay low upon the great city. Mud-colored clouds drooped sadly over the muddy streets. Down the Strand the lamps were but misty splotches of diffused light which threw a feeble circular glimmer upon the slimy pavement. The yellow glare from the shop-windows streamed out into the steamy, vaporous air, and threw a murky, shifting radiance across the crowded thoroughfare. There was, to my mind, something eerie and ghost-like in the endless procession of faces which flitted across these narrow bars of light,--sad faces and glad, haggard and merry. Like all human kind, they flitted from the gloom into the light, and so back into the gloom once more. I am not subject to impressions, but the dull, heavy evening, with the strange business upon which we were engaged, combined to make me nervous and depressed. I could see from Miss Morstan's manner that she was suffering from the same feeling. Holmes alone could rise superior to petty influences. He held his open note-book upon his knee, and from time to time he jotted down figures and memoranda in the light of his pocket-lantern.

At the Lyceum Theatre the crowds were already thick at the side-entrances. In front a continuous stream of hansoms and four-wheelers were rattling up, discharging their cargoes of shirt-fronted men and beshawled, bediamonded women. We had hardly reached the third pillar, which was our rendezvous, before a small, dark, brisk man in the dress of a coachman accosted us.

4 THE STORY OF THE BALD-HEADED MAN

Chapter Four

There is a certain amount of horror in the scene that follows, as 'a blaze of yellow light' streams out, reminiscent of some similarly-coloured scenes from Frankenstein (22).

Their host is 'a small man with 'a bald shining scalp which' shoots out of his 'bristle of red hair' 'like a mountain-peak from fir-trees' (22). His description relates directly to the title of the chapter: 'The Story of the Bald-headed Man' (22). We quickly get the idea that the host is mentally unstable as 'his features' are 'in a perpetual jerk' (22).

The 30-year-old describes his home as 'an oasis of art in the howling desert of South London' (22). By saying this, he displays considerable vanity. The reader must feel his portrayal is extremely unsympathetic.

He introduces himself as 'Thaddeus Sholto' and asks Doctor Watson to check his 'mitral valve' (23). Watson can only gauge that Thaddeus is 'in an ecstasy of fear', which is almost an oxymoron (23). The impression is that Thaddeus virtually enjoys being afraid, as if he has masochist tendencies.

Thaddeus makes his brother sound like an intimidating person and he warns the group that 'nothing would annoy Brother Bartholomew more than any publicity' (23).

When Thaddeus blinks his 'weak, watery blue eyes' it reminds us of his lack of physical strength (24) However, the reader may distrust Thaddeus professed 'shrinking from all forms of rough materialism', given that he is surrounded by opulence and riches (24).

Watson suggests that they should set off immediately to Norwood to 'see Brother Bartholomew' given the later hour, but Thaddeus laughs 'until his ears' are 'quite red' (25). This shows that Thaddeus is quite contemptuous of other as he seems to look down condescendingly on Watson's quite sensible suggestion.

Thaddeus relates the story of his father, who admitted on his death bed that he had been afflicted by a 'cursed greed' that prevented him from sharing 'the treasure' with Miss Morstan. The reader may imagine that, like his father, Thaddeus may be guilty of 'avarice' (26).

Thaddeus's father claimed on his death bed that Captain Morstan had always had 'a weak heart', which makes the reader think there may be a family connection to Thaddeus and his 'mitral valve' (27, 23). It is claimed that the Captain 'sprung out of his chair' as they argued over 'the treasure' and fell cutting his head (27). Thaddeus's father kept the subsequent death secret for fear of being accused of murder.

Just when Thaddeus's father was about to tell his sons where the treasure was hidden, 'a bearded, hairy face, with cruel eyes' was seen peering through the window (28). Initially, the only evidence the twins can find is 'a single foot-mark' in 'the flower bed' (28). Later, 'a torn piece of paper with the words "The sign of the four" scrawled across it' was found' (28, 29).

Like a stereotypical Victorian female, Miss Morstan is 'about to faint', after hearing this account (29). By contrast, the heroic Holmes is leaning back 'with an abstracted expression' (29). Holmes is clearly fascinated by the case, as his eyes are described as 'glittering' (29).

Thaddeus, meanwhile, speaks in French, which translated means: 'Bad taste leads to crime' (30). It reminds the reader that his 'oasis' may be considered by some to be in bad taste. Perhaps this is a clue leading us to the real criminal, which we may suspect is Thaddeus.

As they prepare to go out, 'no part of' Thaddeus is 'visible save his mobile and peaky face' (31). This indicates that metaphorically he may be hiding the truth. There is nothing honest nor wholesome about his presentation. The idea that he is a 'hyperchondriac' is repeated throughout the chapter, making the reader distrust him (32).

Thaddeus has taken over the narrative for much of this chapter, and this is further embedded by the use of his father as narrator. As in 'Frankenstein', the writer uses embedded narratives to add tension and mystery to the plot.

Starting with this extract, explore how Conan Doyle creates a sense of decadence and decay.
Write about:
• how Conan Doyle creates a sense of decadence and decay in this extract
• how Conan Doyle creates a sense of decadence and decay in the novel as a whole.

[30 marks]

We followed the Indian down a sordid and common passage, ill-lit and worse furnished, until he came to a door upon the right, which he threw open. A blaze of yellow light streamed out upon us, and in the centre of the glare there stood a small man with a very high head, a bristle of red hair all round the fringe of it, and a bald, shining scalp which shot out from among it like a mountain-peak from fir-trees. He writhed his hands together as he stood, and his features were in a perpetual jerk -- now smiling, now scowling, but never for an instant in repose. Nature had given him a pendulous lip, and a too visible line of yellow and irregular teeth, which he strove feebly to conceal by constantly passing his hand over the lower part of his face. In spite of his obtrusive baldness he gave the impression of youth. In point of fact, he had just turned his thirtieth year.

"Your servant, Miss Morstan," he kept repeating in a thin, high voice. "Your servant, gentlemen. Pray step into my little sanctum. A small place, miss, but furnished to my own liking. An oasis of art in the howling desert of South London."

We were all astonished by the appearance of the apartment into which he invited us. In that sorry house it looked as out of place as a diamond of the first water in a setting of brass. The richest and glossiest of curtains and tapestries draped the walls, looped back here and there to expose some richly mounted painting or Oriental vase. The carpet was of amber and black, so soft and so thick that the foot sank pleasantly into it, as into a bed of moss. Two great tiger-skins thrown athwart it increased the suggestion of Eastern luxury, as did a huge hookah which stood upon a mat in the corner. A lamp in the fashion of a silver dove was hung from an almost invisible golden wire in the centre of the room. As it burned it filled the air with a subtle and aromatic odour.

"Mr. Thaddeus Sholto," said the little man, still jerking and smiling. "That is my name. You are Miss Morstan, of course. And these gentlemen --"

AO1 - Personal response
AO2 - Writer's effect
AO3 – Context

5 THE TRAGEDY OF PONDICHERRY LODGE

Chapter Five

The chapter is entitled: 'The Tragedy of Pondicherry Lodge' and, by 11pm, they reach the place mentioned (33). The title warns us to expect something awful and this is further foreshadowed by 'half a moon peeping' through 'heavy clouds' (33). This seems the perfect setting for some unspeakable gothic crime.

The building is 'vast' and, with 'its gloom and its deadly silence', it strikes 'a chill to the heart' (34). Bartholomew's window is 'where the moonlight strikes', highlighting a possible place where something heinous has been committed (34). Using the sound imagery of the housekeeper, Mrs Bernstein, 'whimpering', the narrator conveys to that something awful has indeed happened (34).

Meanwhile, the horror of the situation draws Miss Morstan closer to Watson, as he discovers 'her hand' in his (34). He thinks it is 'instinct' that has made her 'turn' to him 'for comfort' (35). Unlike Holmes, he is forever looking for emotional explanations for behaviour.

Holmes remains in control of the situation and never lets his emotions get the better of him. While Thaddeus's teeth are 'chattering', Holmes is looking for evidence with 'his lens'

(37). Watson assists Thaddeus, whose knees are 'trembling', but Holmes is only focused on solving the case (37).

'Moonlight' illuminates the death scene, as we see the grisly smiling face of a recently deceased Batholomew through the keyhole (38). This method of viewing the scene makes it all the more mysterious, as Holmes and Watson can only see part of the room until they break the door down.

Once inside, they can see 'a peculiar instrument - a brown, close-grained stick, with a stone head like a hammer, rudely lashed on with coarse twine' (39). At this stage, it is difficult to imagine exactly how this implement was used in the murder, but the reader trusts that Holmes will work out how it fits into the crime scene. Unsurprisingly, a note with 'the sign of the four' written on it is read there. Less predictably, the dead man has 'what looked like a long dark thorn stuck in his skin just above the war' (39). Holmes informs Watson that the thorn is 'poisoned' (39).

Then Thaddeus's cries out that: 'The treasure is gone!' (39). He claims he left Bartholomew at 'ten o'clock' and that now the police will blame him for the murder as he was the last one to see him (40). Strangely, Holmes reassures Thaddeus, telling him: 'You have no reason for fear, Mr Sholto' (40). This is uncharacteristic of Holmes, as earlier in the novel he tells Watson that 'a client is a [...] mere unit, a factor in a problem' (40). Suddenly, he seems less like the automaton that Watson accused him of being, and more like a human being.

Starting with this extract, explore how Conan Doyle uses the gothic genre to engage the reader.
Write about:
• how Conan Doyle uses the gothic genre in this extract
• how Conan Doyle uses the gothic genre in the novel as a whole.

[30 marks]

"There is something devilish in this, Watson," said he, more moved than I had ever before seen him. "What do you make of it?"

I stooped to the hole and recoiled in horror. Moonlight was streaming into the room, and it was bright with a vague and shifty radiance. Looking straight at me and suspended, as it were, in the air, for all beneath was in shadow, there hung a face -- the very face of our companion Thaddeus. There was the same high, shining head, the same circular bristle of red hair, the same bloodless countenance. The features were set, however, in a horrible smile, a fixed and unnatural grin, which in that still and moonlit room was more jarring to the nerves than any scowl or contortion. So like was the face to that of our little friend that I looked round at him to make sure that he was indeed with us. Then I recalled to mind that he had mentioned to us that his brother and he were twins.

"This is terrible!" I said to Holmes. "What is to be done?"

"The door must come down," he answered, and springing against it, he put all his weight upon the lock.

It creaked and groaned but did not yield. Together we flung ourselves upon it once more, and this time it gave way with a sudden snap, and we found ourselves within Bartholomew Sholto's chamber.

It appeared to have been fitted up as a chemical laboratory. A double line of glass-stoppered bottles was drawn up upon the wall opposite the door, and the table was littered over with Bunsen burners, test-tubes, and retorts. In the corners stood carboys of acid in wicker baskets. One of these appeared to leak or to have been broken, for a stream of dark-coloured liquid had trickled out from it, and the air was heavy with a peculiarly pungent, tarlike odour. A set of steps stood at one side of the room in the midst of a litter of lath and plaster, and above them there was an opening in the ceiling large enough for a man to pass through. At the foot of the steps a long coil of rope was thrown carelessly together.

By the table in a wooden armchair the master of the house was seated all in a heap, with his head sunk upon his left shoulder and that ghastly, inscrutable smile upon his face. He was stiff and cold and had clearly been dead many hours. It seemed to me that not only his features but all his limbs were twisted and turned in the most fantastic fashion. By his hand upon the table there lay a peculiar instrument -- a brown, close-grained stick, with a stone head like a hammer, rudely lashed on with coarse twine. Beside it was a torn sheet of note-paper with some words scrawled upon it. Holmes glanced at it and then handed it to me.

AO1 - Personal response
AO2 - Writer's effect
AO3 - Context

6 SHERLOCK HOLMES GIVES A DEMONSTRATION

Chapter Six

We learn a little more about Holmes's character at the beginning of this chapter, entitled 'Sherlock Holmes Gives a Demonstration' (41). He displays a superior attitude when telling Watson to 'just sit in the corner' (41). While he clearly values Watson's companionship, he doesn't treat him like an equal.

The narrative switches to the present tense, adding tension, as Holmes explains that the 'wooden-legged' suspect was aided by an 'ally' (42). He tells Watson that 'this ally breaks fresh ground in the annals of crime in this country' (42). By contrast, Holmes uses the past tense to describe the one-legged suspect, which makes him sound less dangerous as the threat is less immediate.

He continues to talk to Watson, as a teacher would to a pupil, saying: 'How often have I said to you that when you have eliminated the impossible, whatever remains, however improbable, must be the truth?' (43). Through the use of this rhetorical question, Holmes mildly scolds Watson.

The narrator compares Holmes to a bird, with his 'long thin nose' and his 'beady eyes gleaming' (44). Perhaps it refers to the detective's ability to pick the wheat from the chaff: an essential gift when choosing which clues to follow-up. Holmes has to be careful not to spend time on red herrings, or irrelevant clues.

Watson is useful to him, though, to confirm what he believes. Holmes uses him as a sounding board. For instance, when he asks his 'conclusion' as to the cause of Bartholomew's death (45). Watson replies that it was caused by 'some vegetable alkaloid' (45). He adds it was from 'some strychnine-like substance which would produce tetanus' (45). Holmes said that occurred to him 'the instant' he 'saw the drawn muscles of the face' (45). Once again, Holmes retains the upper hand in his dealings with his companion.

The next character we are introduced to is a police detective called Athelney Jones. He is described as a 'very stout, portly man in a grey suit' and seems to be the opposite of Holmes (46). Jones repeats himself, by saying: 'Here's a business' and then by saying: 'Here's a pretty business' (46). His method of detection is 'common sense', so he is worlds apart from Holmes, who is much more scientific in his approach (46).

Holmes is clearly more sophisticated than the 'fat detective' as, like Thaddeus, he can speak French (47). The translation of Holmes's French phrase is: 'There are no fools so troublesome as those that have some wit'. Holmes is quoting Francois de la Rochefoucauld, a French nobleman, with whom he shares the view that human conduct should neither be condemned nor celebrated. In keeping with his love of science, he thinks behavior should be observed in a detached, emotionless manner. However, Holmes is observing that Jones is an idiot, who is not completely devoid of intelligence and that makes him a nuisance at times.

Jones refers to Holmes dismissively as 'Mr Theorist', when the latter reassures Thaddeus that he will be able to 'clear' him 'of the charge' of murder (48). It is obvious from this comment that Jones thinks of himself as more practical than Holmes. Nevertheless, Holmes informs Jones of the identity of the suspected one-legged man: 'Jonathan Small' (48).

Holmes has no confidence in Jones's ability to find the real murderer, as he suggests leaving him 'to exult over any mare's nest which he may choose to construct' (49). The 'mare's nest' expression refers to someone's ability to discover something seemingly amazing, which doesn't actually exist. However, Holmes does believe in old Sherman's dog, Toby, so sends Watson off to bring back the 'queer mongrel' (49).

Before Watson heads off, Holmes quotes the 'pithy' German philosopher Goethe. The translation is: 'We are used to seeing that Man despises what he never comprehends' (50). It clearly refers to Jones, wrongly accusing Thaddeus, perhaps because of his exotic appearance which defies understanding. It seems to convey the message that we should not judge a book by its cover, although many Victorians would have been suspicious of someone like Thaddeus with his foreign tastes. By quoting a German philosopher, Holmes is championing being open-minded to continental ideas.

Starting with this extract, explore how Conan Doyle portrays crime and punishment.
Write about:
- **how Conan Doyle portrays crime and punishment in this extract**
- **how Conan Doyle portrays crime and punishment in the novel as a whole.**

[30 marks]

As he spoke, the steps which had been coming nearer sounded loudly on the passage, and a very stout, portly man in a gray suit strode heavily into the room. He was red-faced, burly, and plethoric, with a pair of very small twinkling eyes which looked keenly out from between swollen and puffy pouches. He was closely followed by an inspector in uniform and by the still palpitating Thaddeus Sholto.

"Here's a business!" he cried in a muffled, husky voice. "Here's a pretty business! But who are all these? Why, the house seems to be as full as a rabbit-warren!"

"I think you must recollect me, Mr. Athelney Jones," said Holmes quietly.

"Why, of course I do!" he wheezed. "It's Mr. Sherlock Holmes, the theorist. Remember you! I'll never forget how you lectured us all on causes and inferences and effects in the Bishopgate jewel case. It's true you set us on the right track; but you'll own now that it was more by good luck than good guidance."

"It was a piece of very simple reasoning."

"Oh, come, now, come! Never be ashamed to own up. But what is all this? Bad business! Bad business! Stern facts here -- no room for theories. How lucky that I happened to be out at Norwood over another case! I was at the station when the message arrived. What d'you think the man died of?"

"Oh, this is hardly a case for me to theorize over," said Holmes dryly.

"No, no. Still, we can't deny that you hit the nail on the head sometimes. Dear me! Door locked, I understand. Jewels worth half a million missing. How was the window?"

"Fastened; but there are steps on the sill."

"Well, well, if it was fastened the steps could have nothing to do with the matter. That's common sense. Man might have died in a fit; but then the jewels are missing. Ha! I have a theory. These flashes come upon me at times. -- Just step outside, Ser- geant, and you, Mr. Sholto. Your friend can remain. -- What do you think of this, Holmes? Sholto was, on his own confession, with his brother last night. The brother died in a fit, on which Sholto walked off with the treasure? How's that?"

AO1 - Personal response
AO2 - Writer's effect
AO3 – Context

7 THE EPISODE OF THE BARREL

Chapter Seven

This chapter is entitled: 'The Episode of the Barrel', so we can expect this object to be instrumental, at least, in this part of the story (51).

However, it begins with Watson revealing his reluctance to take advantage of Miss Morstan's 'weeping' (51). He says it was 'the effort of self-restraint' which held him back. He seems a perfect gentleman, an excellent foil for a stereotypical Victorian woman.

When he leaves Miss Morstan with her employer, Mrs Cecil Forrester, he describes the pair as 'two graceful, clinging figures' illuminated by 'the hall-light shining through stained glass' (52). It shows the pair in a holy light, suggesting purity.

Then we meet Mr Sherman, who is described as 'a lanky, lean old man with stooping shoulders, a stringy neck, and blue-tinted glasses' (53). Reading between the lines we can guess that he is hard-working, which has the 'stooping shoulders', but mildly eccentric, judging by the blue lenses.

Holmes, meanwhile, makes it clear that he is on Thaddeus's side, as he calls him 'friend' (54). He is clearly disgusted with Jones's arrest of Thaddeus, 'the gatekeeper, the housekeeper, and the Indian servant' (54). Taking the police sergeant's 'bull's eye', or small lantern, Holmes tries to get to the bottom of the mystery (54).

He asks Watson to 'loose the dog, and look out for Blondin', referring to the nineteenth-century escapologist, who was a famous tightrope walker (55). Adding to Holmes's magical aura is Watson comment that he's 'like an enormous glow-worm (55).

The dog is also revered for his ability to sniff out a criminal. Watson says that he's 'like a connoisseur sniffling the bouquet of a famous vintage' (56).

The setting the dog leads them to is incredibly depressing, 'with its scattered dirt-heaps and ill-grown shrubs', which have 'a blighted, ill-omened look' (57). All is decay, which is a common theme of turn-of-the-century (fin de siècle) literature.

Holmes reveals that 'Jonathan Small did not get the treasure because he and his associates were themselves convicts' (58). He explains that Major Sholto was 'happy in the possession of the treasure' until he received a letter 'to say that the men whom he had wronged' were no longer in prison (58). Holmes arrogantly says that 'it is the only hypothesis which covers all the facts' (58).

He goes on to explain how Small, who is incredibly small-minded, wanted to regain 'his rights' to the treasure and get 'revenge on the man who had wronged him' (59). He left the 'sign' to show the act of murder was 'something in the nature of an act of justice' (59).

He believes that Small was aided by the 'butler, Lal Rao' (59). He adds that Mrs Bernstone gives Rao 'far from a good character' (59). This seems strangely unscientific of Holmes, who is not usually prone to jumping to conclusions.

Indeed, he is more of a philosopher, proved when he asks Watson if he is 'well up' in his studies of 'Jean Paul' Richter (60). Holmes goes on to cite Richter's idea that 'the chief proof of man's real greatness lies in his perception of his own smallness' (61). This suggests that egotism has no place for the truly great people of this world, but in Holmes's case concerns his considerable eye for detail.

Eventually, Toby the dog leads them to a 'barrel', which causes the narrator and Holmes to 'burst simultaneously into an uncontrollable fit of laughter' (62). On the surface, it seems that the intervention of the dog has yielded no results, at this stage. The reader wonder what exactly this means, so the chapter is ended on a cliffhanger of sorts.

Starting with this extract, explore how Conan Doyle uses setting to enhance the sense of mystery.
Write about:
- **how Conan Doyle uses setting to enhance the sense of mystery in this extract**
- **how Conan Doyle uses setting to enhance the sense of mystery in the novel as a whole.**

[30 marks]

It was nearly two o'clock when we reached Mrs. Cecil Forrester's. The servants had retired hours ago, but Mrs. Forrester had been so interested by the strange message which Miss Morstan had received that she had sat up in the hope of her return. She opened the door herself, a middle-aged, graceful woman, and it gave me joy to see how tenderly her arm stole round the other's waist and how motherly was the voice in which she greeted her. She was clearly no mere paid dependant, but an honored friend. I was introduced, and Mrs. Forrester earnestly begged me to step in and tell her our adventures. I explained, however, the importance of my errand, and promised faithfully to call and report any progress which we might make with the case. As we drove away I stole a glance back, and I still seem to see that little group on the step, the two graceful, clinging figures, the half-opened door, the hall light shining through stained glass, the barometer, and the bright stair-rods. It was soothing to catch even that passing glimpse of a tranquil English home in the midst of the wild, dark business which had absorbed us.

And the more I thought of what had happened, the wilder and darker it grew. I reviewed the whole extraordinary sequence of events as I rattled on through the silent gas-lit streets. There was the original problem: that at least was pretty clear now. The death of Captain Morstan, the sending of the pearls, the advertisement, the letter,--we had had light upon all those events. They had only led us, however, to a deeper and far more tragic mystery. The Indian treasure, the curious plan found among Morstan's baggage, the strange scene at Major Sholto's death, the rediscovery of the treasure immediately followed by the murder of the discoverer, the very singular accompaniments to the crime, the footsteps, the remarkable weapons, the words upon the card, corresponding with those upon Captain Morstan's chart,--here was indeed a labyrinth in which a man less singularly endowed than my fellow-lodger might well despair of ever finding the clue.

Pinchin Lane was a row of shabby two-storied brick houses in the lower quarter of Lambeth. I had to knock for some time at No. 3 before I could make my impression. At last, however, there was the glint of a candle behind the blind, and a face looked out at the upper window.

8 THE BAKER STREET IRREGULARS

Chapter Eight

It is almost as if the dog is Holmes's gothic double, as Watson notes: 'Toby has lost his character for infallibility' (63). By trusting the dog's instincts, Holmes has taken Watson on a wild goose chase. However, Holmes will not give up.

He has a huge ego, which means he underestimates others. This is proven when he says: 'These fellows are sharper than I expected' (64).

As the pair follow the dog chasing a different scent trail to the river, they encounter Mrs Smith and her son, Jack. From her, they discover that the 'wooden-legged man' is a 'monkey-faced chap' with a 'voice, which is kind o' thick and foggy' (65). This description associates this criminal with mysterious weather, where nothing is clear.

Holmes explains that to get information from 'people of that sort' you must 'never let them' know that what they've said is valuable to you, or they 'will instantly shut up like an oyster' (66). This simile conveys the idea that the Smiths are a seafaring family. Additionally, we become aware of Holmes condescending attitude to the lower classes, when he says 'people of that sort'.

He displays the same attitude in his dealings with 'The Baker Street Irregulars', who the chapter is named after. He describes Wiggins, the leader of the group as his 'dirty little lieutenant' (67).

Meanwhile, Watson explains his dilemma. Being a moral man, he chooses to follow the righteous path of trying to deliver 'the treasure' to Miss Morstan, although he admits that if he finds it, it will 'probably put her forever beyond' his reach (68). He believes that as a rich heiress, she will be inundated with suitors and he will have no chance of winning her love.

We then meet 'the ragged little street Arabs', who are the aforementioned 'unofficial' child police force of Baker Street 'irregulars'. Wiggins is described as 'a disreputable little scarecrow' by the narrator. This makes it clear that Watson has little regard for Holmes's young allies.

After the irregulars are sent on their mission to 'find the whereabouts of a steam launch called "Aurora"', Holmes begins explaining who is responsible for the 'diminutive foot-marks' at the scene of the crime (70, 71). He says that a 'savage' from the 'Andaman Islands' must have fired the dart from 'a blow pipe' into

Bartholomew's neck (71). The word 'savage' is offensive to modern readers, due to the inherent racism implied. However, during Victorian times, many readers would have not thought the term to be derisory.

Holmes reads to Watson from his latest 'gazetteer', which shows he is quite erudite and well-informed for his time (71). He quotes the book to inform Watson that: 'The aborigines of the Andaman Islands may perhaps claim the distinction of being the smallest race upon this earth' (72).

After all this mental work, Holmes takes 'up his violin' (72). This proves he is a genius in more than one field, as in music also he shows 'a remarkable gift for improvisation' (73).

Starting with this extract, explore how Conan Doyle conveys imperialist attitudes. Write about:
- **how Conan Doyle conveys imperialist attitudes in this extract**
- **how Conan Doyle conveys imperialist attitudes in the novel as a whole.**

[30 marks]

"A savage!" I exclaimed. "Perhaps one of those Indians who were the associates of Jonathan Small."

"Hardly that," said he. "When first I saw signs of strange weapons I was inclined to think so; but the remarkable character of the footmarks caused me to reconsider my views. Some of the inhabitants of the Indian Peninsula are small men, but none could have left such marks as that. The Hindoo proper has long and thin feet. The sandal-wearing Mohammedan has the great toe well separated from the others, because the thong is commonly passed between. These little darts, too, could only be shot in one way. They are from a blow-pipe. Now, then, where are we to find our savage?"

"South American," I hazarded.

He stretched his hand up, and took down a bulky volume from the shelf. "This is the first volume of a gazetteer which is now being published. It may be looked upon as the very latest authority. What have we here? 'Andaman Islands, situated 340 miles to the north of Sumatra, in the Bay of Bengal.' Hum! hum! What's all this? Moist climate, coral reefs, sharks, Port Blair, convict-barracks, Rutland Island, cottonwoods-- Ah, here we are. 'The aborigines of the Andaman Islands may perhaps claim the distinction of being the smallest race upon this earth, though some anthropologists prefer the Bushmen of Africa, the Digger Indians of America, and the Terra del Fuegians. The average height is rather below four feet, although many full-grown adults may be found who are very much smaller than this. They are a fierce, morose, and intractable people, though capable of forming most devoted friendships when their confidence has once been gained.' Mark that, Watson. Now, then, listen to this. 'They are naturally hideous, having large, misshapen heads, small, fierce eyes, and distorted features. Their feet and hands, however, are remarkably small. So intractable and fierce are they that all the efforts of the British official have failed to win them over in any degree. They have always been a terror to shipwrecked crews, braining the survivors with their stone-headed clubs, or shooting them with their poisoned arrows. These massacres are invariably concluded by a cannibal feast.' Nice, amiable people, Watson! If this fellow had been left to his own unaided devices this affair might have taken an even more ghastly turn. I fancy that, even as it is, Jonathan Small would give a good deal not to have employed him."

9 A BREAK IN THE CHAIN

Chapter Nine

We see Holmes's commitment to a lifelong education again, as he is 'deep in a book', when Watson awakes at the start of the chapter entitled: 'A Break in the Chain' (74).

Watson is shocked by Holmes's sexist misogyny, as he warns his friend that 'women are never to be entirely trusted' (74). Watson calls it an 'atrocious sentiment', emphasizes their difference of opinion on the fairer sex.

Although he is instructed not to reveal too much to Miss Morstan and Mrs Forrester, the latter's comment that the story of Bartholomew's death is 'a romance' suggests he may have given them quite a detailed account (75). Both ladies know that the story includes 'an injured lady, half a million in treasure, a black cannibal, and a wooden-legged ruffian' (75).

Miss Mary Morstan shows 'no sign of elation at the prospect' of becoming rich (75). This shows how virtuous she is, as Watson notes.

Meanwhile, Holmes shows an obsessive side to his character, as he is portrayed walking up and down rather than sleeping at night. As he readily admits, the 'infernal problem is consuming' him (76).

Possibly to take his mind off the case, Holmes busies himself with what Watson calls a 'malodorous chemical experiment' (77). The reader may suspect that this activity has something to do with solving the case.

Later, Holmes changes into 'a rude sailor dress' to go 'down the river' (77). He instructs Watson to 'remain' as his 'representative', as he expects news at any moment (77).

It is clear that Holmes trusts Watson, as he also instructs him 'to act on' his 'own judgement if any news should come' (78). However, nothing initially materialises except a report in the newspaper, revealing that Thaddeus and the housekeeper have been released without charge by the police.

Watson also notes how 'ingenious' Holmes is to put an advertisement in the same paper, asking for information about 'the whereabouts of [...] Mordecai Smith and the launch "Aurora"' (79). By saying that the information is being requested by Mrs Smith, Watson believes that Holmes is disguising the fact that it is he who actual seeks her husband and the boat. However, perhaps some criminals may recognise Holmes's address: '221B, Baker Street, which is also in the advertisement.

A 'downcast' Jones arrives at Baker Street, looking for Holmes, whom he describes as 'a wonderful man' (80). However, the policeman takes 'satisfaction' from the fact that Holmes 'has been at fault too' (81). This suggests a deep rivalry between the two men.

When Holmes turns up in disguise, both Jones and Watson are fooled by his 'aged' appearance, until his normal 'voice' breaks in 'upon' them (81, 82). Jones commends Holmes's impression of a 'workhouse cough', alluding to the miserable conditions endured by the poverty-stricken during the Victorian era (83).

It seems that Holmes is a man of many talents, as he vows to impress Jones and Watson with his 'merits as a housekeeper' (84). This suggests Holmes's extreme versatility and confidence.

Starting with this extract, explore how Conan Doyle explores the theme of wealth. Write about:
• how Conan Doyle explores the theme of wealth in this extract

- **how Conan Doyle explores the theme of wealth in the novel as a whole.**

[30 marks]

I took our mongrel accordingly, and left him, together with a half-sovereign, at the old naturalist's in Pinchin Lane. At Camberwell I found Miss Morstan a little weary after her night's adventures, but very eager to hear the news. Mrs. Forrester, too, was full of curiosity. I told them all that we had done, suppressing, however, the more dreadful parts of the tragedy. Thus, although I spoke of Mr. Sholto's death, I said nothing of the exact manner and method of it. With all my omissions, however, there was enough to startle and amaze them.

"It is a romance!" cried Mrs. Forrester. "An injured lady, half a million in treasure, a black cannibal, and a wooden-legged ruffian. They take the place of the conventional dragon or wicked earl."

"And two knight-errants to the rescue," added Miss Morstan, with a bright glance at me.

"Why, Mary, your fortune depends upon the issue of this search. I don't think that you are nearly excited enough. Just imagine what it must be to be so rich, and to have the world at your feet!"

It sent a little thrill of joy to my heart to notice that she showed no sign of elation at the prospect. On the contrary, she gave a toss of her proud head, as though the matter were one in which she took small interest.

10 THE END OF THE ISLANDER

Chapter Ten

We find out in alliterative terms that the trio's 'meal' is a 'merry one' (85). The repeating 'm' sound suggests music and enjoyment, a radical departure from Holmes's 'black depression' earlier (85).

Holmes reveals that he did indeed plunge himself into 'a chemical analysis' to take his mind off the case (86). This enabled him to consider Small's 'delicate finesse', which he claims 'is usually a product of higher education' (86). His admiration for Small's 'cunning' is clearly growing (86).

Holmes explains that Small would be unlikely to set off immediately in the 'Aurora', as his 'lair would be too valuable' to give up 'until he was sure that he could do without it' (87). The name of the boat foreshadows the idea that there might be a lot of light illuminating the darkness later, like the Northern Lights that it is named after.

While he was in disguise, Holmes reveals that he encountered the boat's owner, Mordecai Smith. Holmes seems to have little regard for him as he describes him as 'the worse for liquor' (88). The detective clearly thinks that Mordecai is like other men of his class, prone to 'chucking shillings about' when he feels 'flush of money' (88). This working class man is being portrayed as a foolish character, who spends his ill-gotten gains on alcohol.

We get the idea that Holmes is a gambler, from his comment that 'it is a hundred to one' that Smith knows where Small and the Islander are (89). Holmes is quite exact with his odds, as he claims that it is 'ten to one that they go downstream' (89). From this we get the impression that Holmes is very calculating and mathematical in his approach to solving mysteries.

This is further emphasised by his insistence that 'you can say with precision what an average number [of people] will be up to', although he admits that 'individuals vary' (90). He has taken on the above theory from his study of Winwood Reade, an author he recommended to Watson earlier.

As the trio and their helpers start their pursuit of the 'Aurora', the pace of the narrative picks up, with the characters beginning to use shorter sentences mixed with imperatives like: 'Full speed ahead, engineer' (90).

Before long 'the dull blur in front of' them turns into 'the dainty "Aurora" (91). This shows literally how the mystery is slowly unravelling as the criminals come into view.

The Islander is unflatteringly described as 'a little black man [...] with a great, misshapen head and a shock of tangled, dishevelled hair' (92). The term 'unhallowed dwarf' makes the Islander appear diabolical, while his 'strong yellow teeth gnashing' suggest he is no more than an animal (92). By dehumanizing the Islander, the writer ensures that the reader has little or no sympathy for him.

The chapter is entitled: 'The End of the Islander', so it is no real surprise when he is shot and falls 'into the stream' (93). Even then, the narrator comments on the Islander's 'venomous, menacing eyes' (94). The reader may wonder whether or not the Islander is actually dead as there is 'no sign' of him thereafter.

Meanwhile, Small gets stuck in the mud-bank and is hauled in 'like some evil fish', along with the two Smiths and the treasure (93). Like the Islander, so far Small has no redeemable characteristics.

Finally, the writer personifies 'the horrible death' that 'passed so close' to Holmes and

Watson 'that night' to emphasise how they flirt with danger. Watson is the more sensitive, as the thought turns him 'sick', while Holmes smiles and shrugs 'his shoulders' (94). This proves how nonchalant Holmes is compared to his sidekick.

Starting with this extract, explore how Conan Doyle adds suspense and tension to the narrative.
Write about:
• how Conan Doyle adds suspense and tension in this extract
• how Conan Doyle adds suspense and tension in the novel as a whole.

[30 marks]

At that moment, however, as our evil fate would have it, a tug with three barges in tow blundered in between us. It was only by putting our helm hard down that we avoided a collision, and before we could round them and recover our way the Aurora had gained a good two hundred yards. She was still, however, well in view, and the murky uncertain twilight was setting into a clear starlit night. Our boilers were strained to their utmost, and the frail shell vibrated and creaked with the fierce energy which was driving us along. We had shot through the Pool, past the West India Docks, down the long Deptford Reach, and up again after rounding the Isle of Dogs. The dull blur in front of us resolved itself now clearly enough into the dainty Aurora. Jones turned our search-light upon her, so that we could plainly see the figures upon her deck. One man sat by the stern, with something black between his knees over which he stooped. Beside him lay a dark mass which looked like a Newfoundland dog. The boy held the tiller, while against the red glare of the furnace I could see old Smith, stripped to the waist, and shovelling coals for dear life. They may have had some doubt at first as to whether we were really pursuing them, but now as we followed every winding and turning which they took there could no longer be any question about it. At Greenwich we were about three hundred paces behind them. At Blackwall we could not have been more than two hundred and fifty. I have coursed many creatures in many countries during my checkered career, but never did sport give me such a wild thrill as this mad, flying man-hunt down the Thames. Steadily we drew in upon them, yard by yard. In the silence of the night we could hear the panting and clanking of their machinery. The man in the stern still crouched upon the deck, and his arms were moving as though he were busy, while every now and then he would look up and measure with a glance the distance which still separated us. Nearer we came and nearer. Jones yelled to them to stop. We were not more than four boat's lengths behind them, both boats flying at a tremendous pace. It was a clear reach of the river, with Barking Level upon one side and the melancholy Plumstead Marshes upon the other. At our hail the man in the stern sprang up from the deck and shook his two clinched fists at us, cursing the while in a high, cracked voice. He was a good-sized, powerful man, and as he stood poising himself with legs astride I could see that from the thigh downwards there was but a wooden stump upon the right side. At the sound of his strident, angry cries there was movement in the huddled bundle upon the deck. It straightened itself into a little black man--the smallest I have ever seen--with a great, misshapen head and a shock of tangled, dishevelled hair. Holmes had already drawn his revolver, and I whipped out mine at the sight of this savage, distorted creature. He was wrapped in some sort of dark ulster or blanket, which left only his face exposed; but that face was enough to give a man a sleepless night. Never have I seen features so deeply marked with all bestiality and cruelty. His small eyes glowed and burned with a sombre light, and his thick lips were writhed back from his teeth, which grinned and chattered at us with a half animal fury.

"Fire if he raises his hand," said Holmes, quietly. We were within a boat's-length by this time, and almost within touch of our quarry. I can see the two of them now as they stood, the white man with his legs far apart, shrieking out curses, and the unhallowed dwarf with his hideous face, and his strong yellow teeth gnashing at us in the light of our lantern.

11 THE GREAT AGRA TREASURE

Chapter Eleven

In this chapter entitled: 'The Great Agra Treasure' we get the point of view of Small (95). He seems motivated by greed, judging by his 'twinkling eyes' that look 'at the box which had been the cause of his ill-doings' (95). Small admits he 'welted' the Islander 'with the slack end of the rope' for killing Bartholomew, which sounds quite barbaric (95). This was because he 'had no quarrel whatever' with 'this young Sholto' (96).

Meanwhile, Jones is a self-congratulatory mood now that Small is in handcuffs and the case seems to have been resolved. Watson notes that Jones 'was already beginning to give himself airs on the strength of the capture' (97).

When Watson goes to deliver the treasure to Miss Morstan, she appears 'dressed in some sort of white diaphanous material' (98). This makes her seem angelic.

Watson seems impetuous in her presence as he tells her that she and Thaddeus 'will have a couple of hundred thousand each' (99). She seems less than impressed though, as there is 'no eagerness in her voice' (99).

When it turns out that the box is 'empty', Watson can contain himself no longer. He explains his joy to Miss Morstan when he says: 'You are within my reach again' (100). He ends the chapter by saying that he 'gained' 'a treasure' as Mary Morstan reciprocates his love.

Starting with this extract, explain how Conan Doyle explores the theme of love. Write about:
- **how Conan Doyle explain how Conan Doyle explores the theme of love in this extract**
- **how Conan Doyle explain how Conan Doyle explores the theme of love in the novel as a whole.**

[30 marks]

"What a pretty box!" she said, stooping over it. This is Indian work, I suppose?"

"Yes; it is Benares metal-work."

And so heavy!" she exclaimed, trying to raise it. "The box alone must be of some value. Where is the key?"

"Small threw it into the Thames," I answered. "I must borrow Mrs. Forrester's poker." There was in the front a thick and broad hasp, wrought in the image of a sitting Buddha. Under this I thrust the end of the poker and twisted it outward as a lever. The hasp sprang open with a loud snap. With trembling fingers I flung back the lid. We both stood gazing in astonishment. The box was empty!

No wonder that it was heavy. The iron-work was two-thirds of an inch thick all round. It was massive, well made, and solid, like a chest constructed to carry things of great price, but not one shred or crumb of metal or jewelry lay within it. It was absolutely and completely empty.

"The treasure is lost," said Miss Morstan, calmly.

As I listened to the words and realized what they meant, a great shadow seemed to pass from my soul. I did not know how this Agra treasure had weighed me down, until now that it was finally removed. It was selfish, no doubt, disloyal, wrong, but I could realize nothing save that the golden barrier was gone from between us. "Thank God!" I ejaculated from my very heart.

She looked at me with a quick, questioning smile. "Why do you say that?" she asked.

"Because you are within my reach again," I said, taking her hand. She did not withdraw it. "Because I love you, Mary, as truly as ever a man loved a woman. Because this treasure, these riches, sealed my lips. Now that they are gone I can tell you how I love you. That is why I said, 'Thank God.'"

"Then I say, 'Thank God,' too," she whispered, as I

drew her to my side. Whoever had lost a treasure, I knew that night that I had gained one.

12 THE STRANGE STORY OF JONATHAN SMALL

Chapter Twelve

Another embedded narrative is about to add a touch more realism to the novel, as the chapter title suggests we will discover more about 'The Strange Story of Jonathan Small' (101).

Small is still a less than sympathetic character, as he is portrayed leaning 'back in his chair' and laughing 'aloud' when Watson shows him the empty box (101). At this stage, the reader may feel that Miss Morstan has been deprived of the treasure that is rightly hers by a depraved criminal.

Apparently, according to Small, the treasure has been 'scattered' in the river (102). Once he drops 'his mask of stoicism', the reader has a chance to find out what has motivated Small to commit these criminal acts (103).

Through his embedded narrative, Small takes the reader back in time to 1857 and the start of the Indian Rebellion, which he calls 'the great mutiny' (104). He had joined the 'Third Buffs', an army regiment on active service in India (103). He calls it a time of 'perfect hell', with 'two hundred thousand black devils let loose' (104). Clearly, for today's reader this language sounds incredibly racist, but even Victorian readers would have had little sympathy for this character, albeit for different reasons.

Small seems to think that the indigenous people of India are inferior, as he describes the country as being 'up like a swarm of bees' (105). Bu comparing them to 'bees' and by using the word 'swarm', Small dehumanises the Indian rebels, making them sound like insects.

The word 'swarming' is used by Small to describe 'the city of Agra', which again suggests that the inhabitants are less than human (106). However, he clearly has a higher regard for his 'Punjabees', whom he describes as 'tall, fierce-looking chaps, Mahomet Singh and Abdullah Khan' (107).

These two 'Sikhs' attack him when he lays his 'musket down to strike a match' and hold him at knife-point and gun-point (108). They tell Small that he must chose to join them or die. Small agrees to join them as long as it is not 'against the safety of the fort' (109). Luckily for him, they want him to help them to secure some 'loot' (109). There seems to be honour amongst thieves, as they swear that the treasure must be 'equally divided among the four' of them (109). The additional person involved is 'Dost Akbar', whom Small has not yet met (109).

Singh and Khan tell Small the story of the 'rajah' and his hoarding of 'gold' (109, 110). They are unhappy with the rajah's unwillingness to take sides in the Indian Rebellion, so are resolved to rob him. The rajah has appointed his 'trusty servant', 'Achmet' to look after the rajah's treasure and to deposit it safely in the fort (110). Khan tells Small that his 'foster-brother Dost Akbar' will lead Achmet 'to a side-postern of the fort' where Singh and Khan will lie in wait (110).

Small says that Achmet's life 'was a thing as light as air' to him (110, 111). Once again, this shows him to be an unrepentant murderer. The reader is unlikely to have any sympathy with such a character.

Through pathetic fallacy, the narrative suggests the enormity of the crime about to take place. Small reveals that 'the rain was falling steadily', indicating that something awful is about to happen (111).

Small describes Achmet as 'a little fat, round fellow', who 'seemed to be all in a quiver with fear' (112). It seems even more merciless and cold-blooded to kill such a weak and helpless man. Even Small admits that 'the more' he 'looked at his fat, frightened face, the harder did it seem that we should slay him in cold blood' (113). However, the thought just makes him want 'to get it over' (113). When Achmet tries to escape, Small trips him and Akbar plunges a 'knife twice in his side' (113).

What perturbs Watson most is the 'flippant and careless way' that Small is narrating his story. The reader is reminded once again, that the crimes Small has committed are heinous (114). The moral seems to be that greed can lead to crime.

We return to Small's narrative, as he explains how they cover Achmet's body 'with loose bricks', which is anything but a decent burial (114). Then the criminals make 'a hollow' in the same hall to put their treasure in (115). They are taking much more care of that than they are with the remains of a human being, who has done nothing wrong.

There is some justice, as the four conspirators are 'arrested as the murderers of Achmet' at the end of the Indian Rebellion (116). However, 'not a word about the jewels came out at the trial, for the rajah had been deposed and driven out of India' (116). Hence, the treasure still has not been recovered by the authorities, who are unaware of its existence.

Small bides his time as a prisoner and is eventually relocated to 'Blair Island in the Andamans' (117). While there, he talks to Major Sholto, who is 'a ruined man' following some heavy losses while playing cards (118). Small asks Sholto whether handing over the 'hidden treasure' will get his 'sentence shortened' (118).

Sholto brings Captain Morstan to Small and asks him to repeat the story. Sholto decides it is 'a private concern' rather than a governmental matter (119) and agrees that he and the captain should share a fifth of the treasure, which comes 'to fifty thousand apiece' (120).

Once Small gives Sholto and Morstan the maps, the Major goes off 'to India but' never comes 'back again' (121). Although it's a case of the pot calling the kettle black, Small calls Sholto a 'villain' (121).

Thereafter, Small is completely consumed with thoughts of vengeance as he admits that 'even the Agra treasure had come to be a smaller thing' in his mind compared to 'the slaying of Sholto' (122).

Around that time, Small befriends a 'little Andaman Islander', who is 'sick to death', called 'Tonga' (122). Small nurses Tonga back to health, who ferries him away from the island.

Once Small returns to England with Tonga, he makes 'friends with someone who' can help him (123). He won't 'name no names', so this part of the account remains a mystery, allowing the reader to guess (123).

Alluding to the infamous Victorian freak shows, Small reveals that he profited from 'exhibiting poor Tonga at fair and other such places as the black cannibal' (124). This shows that Small is no stranger to exploiting others for his own gain.

Small describes Tonga 'as proud as a peacock', after the murder of Bartholomew (124). This suggests again, that he sees the Islander as little more than a crude animal. He goes on to describe him as 'a bloodthirsty little imp', which again reveals how little regard he has for him (125).

After Small finishes his story and heads for prison, Watson reveals his engagement to Miss Morstan. Holmes gives out 'a most dismal groan', which shows how selfish he is (126). Holmes says: 'I really cannot congratulate you' (126). He explains to Watson that 'whatever is emotional is opposed to that true cold reason' which he places above all things (126). Once again, the reader is reminded to align reason with Holmes and emotion with Watson.

The end of the story sees Holmes return to his drug of choice, cocaine. However, before he does that he surmises that Small's 'confederate in the house' was probably Lal Rao and, thinking of himself, quotes Goethe (127). The translation of the quotation is: 'Nature, alas, made only one being out of you although there was material for a good man and a rogue'. These words sum up Holmes's 'Jeckyl and Hyde' nature and indicate he could have ended up as a devious criminal had he not become a detective instead.

Starting with this extract, explain how Conan Doyle explores the theme of the duality of human nature.
Write about:

- how Conan Doyle explain how Conan Doyle explores the theme of the duality of human nature in this extract
- how Conan Doyle explain how Conan Doyle explores the theme of the duality of human nature in the novel as a whole.

[30 marks]

13 AQA-STYLE ASSESSMENTS

AQA-style Specimen Assessment Material 1:
Starting with this extract, explore how Conan Doyle presents criminals in *The Sign of Four*.

THE SIGN OF FOUR – STUDY GUIDE

Write about:
• how does Conan Doyle present the criminal in this extract
• how does Conan Doyle present criminals in the novel as a whole.

EXTRACT

Sir Arthur Conan Doyle: The Sign of Four
Read the following extract from Chapter 11 of The Sign of Four and then answer the question.
In this extract, Holmes is about to talk to Jonathan Small, who has just been arrested for his part in the death of Bartholomew Sholto and the theft of the Agra Treasure. The extract is important for it reveals contemporary attitudes towards criminals.

Our captive sat in the cabin opposite to the iron box which he had done so much and waited so long to gain. He was a sunburned, reckless-eyed fellow, with a net-work of lines and wrinkles all over his mahogany features, which told of a hard, open-air life. There was a singular prominence about his bearded chin which marked a man who was not to be easily turned from his purpose. His age may have been fifty or thereabouts, for his black, curly hair was thickly shot with grey. His face in repose was not an unpleasing one, though his heavy brows and aggressive chin gave him, as I had lately seen, a terrible expression when moved to anger. He sat now with his handcuffed hands upon his lap, and his head sunk upon his breast, while he looked with his keen, twinkling eyes at the box which had been the cause of his ill-doings. It seemed to me that there was more sorrow than anger in his rigid and contained countenance. Once he looked up at me with a gleam of something like humour in his eyes.

"Well, Jonathan Small," said Holmes, lighting a cigar, "I am sorry that it has come to this."

"And so am I, sir," he answered, frankly. "I don't believe that I can swing over the job. I give you my word on the book that I never

Comment [JB(]: AO2 – The word 'captive' reminds us that Small has

Comment [JB(]: AO1 – Small is positioned next to the box that is

Comment [JB(]: AO2 – The repetition of the word 'so' gives the reader gets the

Comment [JB(]: AO1 – If eyes are the windows to the soul, the 'reckless-eyed'

Comment [JB(]: AO2 – The word 'network' reminds readers of how

Comment [JB(]: AO1 – The message here is crime does not pay. All it has led

Comment [JB(]: AO1 – Small's determination is not in question.

Comment [JB(]: AO3 – These physical features tie in with the popular Victorian

Comment [JB(]: AO1 – The writer shows how awful it is for criminals when they

Comment [JB(]: AO2 – The description of his eyes as 'keen' and 'twinkling' imply

Comment [JB(]: AO1 – The writer shows that the criminal is sad, but we cannot be

Comment [JB(]: AO1 – We get the impression that the narrator cannot

Comment [JB(]: AO1 – Despite his capture, Small is respectful to Holmes.

JOE BROADFOOT

raised hand against Mr. Sholto. It was that little hell-hound Tonga who shot one of his cursed darts into him. I had no part in it, sir. I was as grieved as if it had been my blood-relation. I welted the little devil with the slack end of the rope for it, but it was done, and I could not undo it again."

AQA-style Specimen Assessment Material 2:

Starting with this extract, explore how Conan Doyle presents women in *The Sign of Four*.
Write about:
• how does Conan Doyle present women in this extract
• how does Conan Doyle present women in the novel as a whole.

EXTRACT

Sir Arthur Conan Doyle: The Sign of Four
Read the following extract from Chapter 7 of The Sign of Four and then answer the question.
In this extract, Watson is escorting Mary Morstan to her place of work and residence. She is employed as a governess by Mrs Cecil Forrester (who, interestingly, is known formally by her husband's first name). The extract is important for it reveals contemporary attitudes towards women.

It was nearly two o'clock when we reached Mrs. Cecil Forrester's. The servants had retired hours ago, but Mrs. Forrester had been so interested by the strange message which Miss Morstan had received that she had sat up in the hope of her return. She opened the door herself, a middle-aged, graceful woman, and it gave me joy to see how tenderly her arm stole round the other's waist and how motherly was the voice in which she greeted her. She was clearly no mere paid dependant, but an honored friend. I was introduced, and Mrs. Forrester earnestly begged me to step in and tell her our adventures. I explained, however, the importance of my

> Comment [JB(]: AO2 – The alliterative 'hell-hound' emphasises how evil Tonga is in Small's eyes. However, hounds are known for their loyalty, which is not being shown by Small to his accomplice. Small

> Comment [JB(]: AO1 – The idea of honour amongst thieves is lost on Small, who immediately tells Holmes that Tonga is the murderer. The reader may find it hard to believe that Small has no

> Comment [JB(]: AO1 – Although she is Mary Mostan's employer, Mrs Forrester is presented as homely and caring, staying awake later than usual to greet her employee when she returns.

> Comment [JB(]: AO1 – Mrs Forrester has even allowed the servants to go to bed, and has gone to considerable effort to wait for Mary's return. She is portrayed as a kind and warm person.

> Comment [JB(]: AO2 – The adverbs 'tenderly' and 'motherly' add to the impression that Mrs Forrester is a kind, caring and warm person.

> Comment [JB(]: AO1 – The relationship between the two women is much more than simply a working arrangement. Although, Mary works for Mrs Forrester as a governess, a close friendship seems

> Comment [JB(]: AO1 – Mrs Forrester is portrayed as a welcoming hostess to Watson, whom she has never met before. This makes her appear very trusting, albeit it a touch naïve. These qualities

THE SIGN OF FOUR – STUDY GUIDE

errand, and promised faithfully to call and report any progress which we might make with the case. As we drove away I stole a glance back, and I still seem to see that little group on the step, the two graceful, clinging figures, the half opened door, the hall light shining through stained glass, the barometer, and the bright stair-rods. It was soothing to catch even that passing glimpse of a tranquil English home in the midst of the wild, dark business which had absorbed us.

AQA-style Specimen Assessment Material 3:

Starting with this extract, explore how Conan Doyle presents Watson in *The Sign of Four*.
Write about:
• how does Conan Doyle present Watson in this extract
• how does Conan Doyle present Watson in the novel as a whole.

EXTRACT

Sir Arthur Conan Doyle: The Sign of Four
Read the following extract from Chapter 7 of The Sign of Four and then answer the question.
In this extract, Watson is following Holmes instructions to escort Mary Morstan home, not long after the discovery of the murdered Batholomew Sholto. The extract is important for it shows how Watson's emotional involvement in the case gives it a different hue to Holmes, who sees 'a client as a mere unit'.

The police had brought a cab with them, and in this I escorted Miss Morstan back to her home. After the angelic fashion of women, she had borne trouble with a calm face as long as there was some one weaker than herself to support, and I had found her bright and placid by the side of the frightened housekeeper. In the cab, however, she first turned faint, and then burst into a passion of weeping, — so sorely had she been tried by the adventures of the

87

Comment [JB(): AO1 – The implication here is that men's work is more important than women's, although Watson modestly describes his job as 'errand'.

Comment [JB(): AO3 – The image of two helpless women in front of a house holding each other desperately is typical of Victorian fiction, as they appear to

Comment [JB(): AO2 – The writer uses religious imagery to describe the women. The scene gains an almost holy light as the light from the hall streams through

Comment [JB(): AO2 – The juxtaposition of light and dark here flatters these gentlewomen, who seem to be located in an almost holy and 'tranquil' place of

Comment [JB(): AO1 – By applying the word 'angelic' to women in general, Watson conveys the idea that he thinks all females should conform to certain

Comment [JB(): AO1 – Watson's fixation on Mary is obvious, as he observes and admires her strong, but feminine demeanour.

Comment [JB(): AO1 – Once again, Watson conveys his admiration for Mary, who he believes can be strong when she has someone else to look after. For

Comment [JB(): AO2 – The writer uses the soft sound of sibilance to show how Watson is ready to excuse Mary's sobbing in the cab.

night. She has told me since that she thought me cold and distant upon that journey. She little guessed the struggle within my breast or the effort of self-restraint which held me back. My sympathies and my love went out to her, even as my hand had in the garden. I felt that years of the conventionalities of life could not teach me to know her sweet, brave nature as had this one day of strange experiences. Yet there were two thoughts which sealed the words of affection upon my lips. She was weak and helpless, shaken in mind and nerve. It was to take her at a disadvantage to obtrude love upon her at such a time. Worse still, she was rich. If Holmes's researches were successful, she would be an heiress. Was it fair, was it honorable, that a half-pay surgeon should take such advantage of an intimacy which chance had brought about? Might she not look upon me as a mere vulgar fortuneseeker? I could not bear to risk that such a thought should cross her mind. This Agra treasure intervened like an impassable barrier between us.

> Comment [JB(]: AO1 – Watson's revelation that 'she has told me since' reveals that he has maintained some of
>
> Comment [JB(]: AO2 – The metaphor of the 'struggle within' Watson's 'breast' reminds us that this is a matter of the
>
> Comment [JB(]: AO2 – The personification of 'sympathies and love' make it appear as if Watson is completely
>
> Comment [JB(]: AO1 – Watson reminds us that he has already made physical contact with Mary. He clearly is losing the
>
> Comment [JB(]: AO2 – The use of hyperbole implies that Watson is ready to fall in love in 'one day'. He seems to
>
> Comment [JB(]: AO2 – The 'two thoughts' are personified, which gives them even greater importance.
>
> Comment [JB(]: AO3 – Watson wants to a Victorian gentleman in every sense of the word. Therefore to 'obtrude' or force
>
> Comment [JB(]: AO3 – In Victorian times, people were supposed to marry others in a similar socio-economic
>
> Comment [JB(]: AO2 – Using a series of rhetorical questions, Watson persuades himself that he is unworthy of Mary's
>
> Comment [JB(]: AO2 – The simile of the 'impassable barrier' makes the reader realise how important honour and

AQA-style Specimen Assessment Material 4: 'Jonathan Small is a totally unsympathetic character.'
Starting with this extract, how does Conan Doyle present the character of Thaddeus Sholto?
Write about:
• how Conan Doyle presents Thaddeus Sholto in this extract
• how Conan Doyle presents Thaddeus Sholto in the novel as a whole.

EXTRACT

Sir Arthur Conan Doyle: The Sign of Four
Read the following extract from Chapter 4 of The Sign of Four and then answer the question.
In this extract, Holmes, Watson and Mary Morstan meet and speak to Thaddeus Sholto in his not so humble abode. They have travelled through London to get here from the Lyceum Theatre and now they are hoping that Thaddeus, whom they have just met, will help them unravel the mystery. The extract is important as we gain insight into Watson's view of Thaddeus.

THE SIGN OF FOUR – STUDY GUIDE

"Mr. Thaddeus Sholto," said the little man, still jerking and smiling. "That is my name. You are Miss Morstan, of course. And these gentlemen—"

"This is Mr. Sherlock Holmes, and this is Dr. Watson."

"A doctor, eh?" cried he, much excited. "Have you your stethoscope? Might I ask you—would you have the kindness? I have grave doubts as to my mitral valve, if you would be so very good. The aortic I may rely upon, but I should value your opinion upon the mitral."

I listened to his heart, as requested, but was unable to find anything amiss, save indeed that he was in an ecstasy of fear, for he shivered from head to foot. "It appears to be normal," I said. "You have no cause for uneasiness."

"You will excuse my anxiety, Miss Morstan," he remarked, airily. "I am a great sufferer, and I have long had suspicions as to that valve. I am delighted to hear that they are unwarranted. Had your father, Miss Morstan, refrained from throwing a strain upon his heart, he might have been alive now."

I could have struck the man across the face, so hot was I at this callous and off-hand reference to so delicate a matter. Miss Morstan sat down, and her face grew white to the lips. "I knew in my heart
that he was dead," said she.

"I can give you every information," said he, "and, what is more, I can do you justice; and I will, too, whatever Brother Bartholomew may say. I am so glad to have your friends here, not only as an escort to you, but also as witnesses to what I am about to do and say. The three of us can show a bold front to Brother Bartholomew. But let us have no outsiders,—no police or officials. We can settle everything satisfactorily among ourselves, without any interference. Nothing would annoy Brother Bartholomew more

> **Comment [JB():** AO2 – The –ing form of both verbs makes it appear that Thaddeus is continually 'jerking and smiling'. It appears that he of a nervous disposition.

> **Comment [JB():** AO1 – We quickly discover Thaddeus is a hypochondriac, as he immediately wants Watson to examine him.
> AO2 – Thaddeus uses technical language, which makes him seem aware of various heart conditions. Only a well-informed individual would know the difference between an aortic and mitral valve.

> **Comment [JB():** AO2 – The word 'ecstasy' is usually a positive word, where 'fear' is anything but. Therefore, this works an oxymoron to show how confused Thaddeus is. On the one hand, he seems to like the excitement, on the other, he is struggling with the strain of it.

> **Comment [JB():** AO1 – As we see the action mostly through Watson's eyes, we are unlikely to warm to Thaddeus's character, especially after this outburst, which makes him appear insensitive.

> **Comment [JB():** AO1 – Thaddeus appears to be much weaker than his brother, if we believe his testimony.

> **Comment [JB():** AO2 – The use of negative language shows how Thaddeus is scared of the law and anything outside of his sphere of influence.

than any publicity." He sat down upon a low settee and blinked at us inquiringly with his weak, watery blue eyes.

> Comment [JB(]: AO2 – The fact that Thaddeus is sitting on a 'low' settee implies that he could be immoral, as he is positioned nearer the devil that God.
> AO3 – His moral could be questionable by Victorian standards, as his character bears a marked resemblance to Conan Doyle's contemporary, Oscar Wilde.

AQA-style Specimen Assessment Material 5:
Starting with this extract, explore the ideas conveyed by Conan Doyle about Holmes's character through his dealings with 'ordinary people' in *The Sign of Four*.
Write about:
• how does Conan Doyle convey ideas about Holmes's character through his dealings with 'ordinary people' in this extract
• how does Conan Doyle convey ideas about Holmes's character through his dealings with 'ordinary people' in the novel as a whole.

EXTRACT

Sir Arthur Conan Doyle: The Sign of Four
Read the following extract from Chapter 8 of The Sign of Four and then answer the question.

In this extract, Holmes is talking to Mrs Smith, Mordecai's wife, about the 'Aurora' and her husband. The extract is important for it reveals contemporary attitudes towards the lower classes.

But, my dear Mrs. Smith," said Holmes, shrugging his shoulders, "You are frightening yourself about nothing. How could you possibly tell that it was the wooden-legged man who came in the night? I don't quite understand how you can be so sure."

"His voice, sir. I knew his voice, which is kind o' thick and foggy. He tapped at the winder,—about three it would be. 'Show a leg, matey,' says he: 'time to turn out guard.' My old man woke up Jim,—that's my eldest,—and away they went, without so much as a word to me. I could hear the wooden leg clackin' on the stones."

> Comment [JB(]: AO2 – Thaddeus appears to be a physically fragile character, judging by his 'weak, watery' eyes.

> Comment [JB(]: AO1 – Holmes's adopts a benign but patronising tone with a working-class woman.

> Comment [JB(]: AO2 – Holmes uses a rhetorical question to show how ridiculous Mrs Smith is being.

> Comment [JB(]: AO2 – The author writes phonetically here to show Mrs Smith's accent and imply a lack of education.
> AO3 – Free elementary education was only provided from 1891, the year after 'The Sign of Four' was published.

THE SIGN OF FOUR – STUDY GUIDE

"And was this wooden-legged man alone?"

"Couldn't say, I am sure, sir. I didn't hear no one else."

> **Comment [JB():** AO2 – The writer portrays Mrs Smith as uneducated through her lack of grammar and the use of a double negative.

"I am sorry, Mrs. Smith, for I wanted a steam launch, and I have heard good reports of the—Let me see, what is her name?"

"The Aurora, sir."

> **Comment [JB():** AO3 – The class system is apparent, as Mrs Smith addresses Holmes as 'sir', whereas he does not refer to her as 'madam' or 'miss'.

"Ah! She's not that old green launch with a yellow line, very broad in the beam?"

"No, indeed. She's as trim a little thing as any on the river. She's been fresh painted, black with two red streaks."

> **Comment [JB():** AO2 – Mrs Smith continues to use poor grammar, this time not using an adverb correctly. This again portrays her as poorly educated.

"Thanks. I hope that you will hear soon from Mr. Smith. I am going down the river, and if I should see anything of the Aurora I shall let him know that you are uneasy. A black funnel, you say?"

> **Comment [JB():** AO2 – Holmes's speech includes a semi-colon and lack the contractions that Mrs Smith's dialogue contains. The juxtaposition of the two characters makes Holmes seem superior and well educated in comparison to her.

"No, sir. Black with a white band."

"Ah, of course. It was the sides which were black. Good-morning, Mrs. Smith.—There is a boatman here with a wherry, Watson. We shall take it and cross the river."

> **Comment [JB():** AO3 – The wherry was evolving into a gentleman's form of river transport in the Victorian era. They were later called skiffs. Holmes shows how different he is to the working-class Mrs

"The main thing with people of that sort," said Holmes, as we sat in the sheets of the wherry, "is never to let them think that their information can be of the slightest importance to you. If you do, they will instantly shut up like an oyster. If you listen to them under protest, as it were, you are very likely to get what you want."

> **Comment [JB():** AO1 – Holmes is extremely condescending, dismissive and ready to generalise about the working-classes, when he speaks to Watson (who is from the same social class).

> **Comment [JB():** AO2 – The use of the simile likens the working-classes to the food they used to eat in the nineteenth-century. It has the effect of making them seem cheap and easy to buy, while also

AQA-style Specimen Assessment Material 6:
Starting with this extract, explore the ideas conveyed about the media and the police by Conan Doyle in *The Sign of Four*.
Write about:
• how does Conan Doyle convey ideas about the media and the

JOE BROADFOOT

police in this extract
• how does Conan Doyle convey ideas about the media and the police in the novel as a whole.

EXTRACT

Sir Arthur Conan Doyle: The Sign of Four
Read the following extract from Chapter 8 of The Sign of Four and then answer the question.
In this extract, Holmes and Watson are enjoying breakfast together after the 'successive excitements' of the night before. The extract is important for it reveals contemporary attitudes towards the media and the police.

"Here it is," said he, laughing, and pointing to an open newspaper. "The energetic Jones and the ubiquitous reporter have fixed it up between them. But you have had enough of the case. Better have your ham and eggs first."

I took the paper from him and read the short notice, which was headed "Mysterious Business at Upper Norwood."

"About twelve o'clock last night," said the Standard, "Mr. Bartholomew Sholto, of Pondicherry Lodge, Upper Norwood, was found dead in his room under circumstances which point to foul play. As far as we can learn, no actual traces of violence were found upon Mr. Sholto's person, but a valuable collection of Indian gems which the deceased gentleman had inherited from his father has been carried off. The discovery was first made by Mr. Sherlock Holmes and Dr. Watson, who had called at the house with Mr. Thaddeus Sholto, brother of the deceased. By a singular piece of good fortune, Mr. Athelney Jones, the well-known member of the detective police force, happened to be at the Norwood Police Station, and was on the ground within half an hour of the first alarm. His trained and experienced faculties were at once directed towards the detection of the criminals, with the gratifying result that the brother, Thaddeus Sholto, has already been arrested, together with the housekeeper, Mrs. Bernstone, an Indian butler

92

Comment [JB(]: AO1 – Holmes's cynicism towards both professions is evident in his ironic use of the word 'energetic' and 'ubiquitous'. The unfit policeman Jones is far from energetic and no journalist was at the scene of the crime, so the reporter cannot be 'ubiquitous'.

Comment [JB(]: AO1 – The repetition of Jones's favourite word 'business' shows that the policeman has had a hand in coming up with the headline. The collusion between the two professions is alarming.

Comment [JB(]: AO1 – Holmes and Watson removed the poison dart from the scene of the crime, but the police should have noticed a puncture mark in Bartholomew's neck.
AO3 – This negative portrayal of the police force is a sign of the times, as Victorians generally had very little confidence in them as crime-stoppers or solvers.

Comment [JB(]: AO1 – Like Jones, the reporter believes that 'good fortune' or luck is important when it comes to solving crimes.

Comment [JB(]: AO2 – The complimentary adjectives 'trained and experienced' add to the idea that the reporter is writing this for the benefit of Jones's reputation. However, it is probably true on both counts, although you could say his training and experience

THE SIGN OF FOUR – STUDY GUIDE

named Lal Rao, and a porter, or gatekeeper, named McMurdo. It is quite certain that the thief or thieves were well acquainted with the house, for Mr. Jones's well-known technical knowledge and his powers of minute observation have enabled him to prove conclusively that the miscreants could not have entered by the door or by the window, but must have made their way across the roof of the building, and so through a trap-door into a room which communicated with that in which the body was found. This fact, which has been very clearly made out, proves conclusively that it was no mere haphazard burglary. The prompt and energetic action of the officers of the law shows the great advantage of the presence on such occasions of a single vigorous and masterful mind. We cannot but think that it supplies an argument to those who would wish to see our detectives more decentralized, and so brought into closer and more effective touch with the cases which it is their duty to investigate."

> **Comment [JB(]:** AO1 – The incompetence of both the media and the police is evident here, as the reporter calls the arrests 'gratifying'. The truth is the police have arrested a group of innocent people.
>
> **Comment [JB(]:** AO1 – Once again, the report flatters Jones. Instead of to the policeman, these words could be rightly applied to Holmes.
>
> **Comment [JB(]:** AO2 – It is ironic that the reporter thinks Jones has proved anything 'conclusively', when he has in fact done nothing of the sort. The word is repeated later for effect.
>
> **Comment [JB(]:** AO2 – As readers, we know that only Holmes has a 'masterful mind', so the alliteration works to add unintended humour to the journalist's report.
>
> **Comment [JB(]:** AO3 – The journalist is voicing the concern that as Britain seemingly became smaller, due to the improvement in the country's infrastructure, there was increasing pressure to centralise public services. Unfortunately, the reporter's assertion that Jones is living proof of how efficient local police inspectors can benefit the community is wrong.

AQA-style Specimen Assessment Material 7:
Starting with this extract, explore how Conan Doyle presents the theme of love and romance in *The Sign of Four*.
Write about:
• how does Conan Doyle present the theme of love and romance in this extract
• how does Conan Doyle present the theme of love and romance in the novel as a whole.

EXTRACT

Sir Arthur Conan Doyle: The Sign of Four
Read the following extract from Chapter 2 of The Sign of Four and then answer the question.
In this extract, Watson has the opportunity to speak to Holmes about Mary Morstan, who is just leaving 221B Baker Street. The extract is important for it explores the theme of love and romance, showing that just because the emotional Watson is attracted to her and sees her as the ideal

JOE BROADFOOT

Victorian woman, it does not follow that his close friend, Holmes, will also find her attractive.

"Au revoir," said our visitor, and, with a bright, kindly glance from one to the other of us, she replaced her pearl-box in her bosom and hurried away. Standing at the window, I watched her walking briskly down the street, until the grey turban and white feather were but a speck in the sombre crowd.

"What a very attractive woman!" I exclaimed, turning to my companion.

He had lit his pipe again, and was leaning back with drooping eyelids. "Is she?" he said, languidly.
"I did not observe."

"You really are an automaton,—a calculating machine!" I cried. "There is something positively inhuman in you at times."

He smiled gently. "It is of the first importance," he said, "not to allow your judgment to be biased by personal qualities. A client is to me a mere unit,—a factor in a problem. The emotional qualities are antagonistic to clear reasoning. I assure you that the most winning woman I ever knew was hanged for poisoning three little children for their insurance-money, and the most repellant man of my acquaintance is a philanthropist who has spent nearly a quarter of a million upon the London poor."

"In this case, however—"

"I never make exceptions. An exception disproves the rule. Have you ever had occasion to study character in handwriting? What do you make of this fellow's scribble?"

AQA-style Specimen Assessment Material 8: 'Jonathan Small is a totally unsympathetic character.'

94

THE SIGN OF FOUR – STUDY GUIDE

Starting with this extract, how far do you agree with this statement?
Write about:
• how Conan Doyle presents Jonathan Small in this extract
• how Conan Doyle presents Jonathan Small in the novel as a whole.

EXTRACT

Sir Arthur Conan Doyle: The Sign of Four
Read the following extract from Chapter 12 of The Sign of Four and then answer the question.
In this extract, Jonathan Small is telling Holmes, Watson and Athelney Jones about the murder of the 'pretended merchant', Achmet, and how the treasure, which now lies at the bottom of the Thames, was originally stolen by the members of 'The Sign of Four' (Small, Mahomet Singh, Abdullah Khan and Dost Akba). The extract is important as we gain insight into Watson's point of view of Small, for a brief moment here, in this break in the embedded narrative.

You see, gentlemen, that I am keeping my promise. I am telling you every work of the business just exactly as it happened, whether it is in my favor or not."

He stopped, and held out his manacled hands for the whiskey-and-water which Holmes had brewed for him. For myself, I confess that I had now conceived the utmost horror of the man, not only for this cold-blooded business in which he had been concerned, but even more for the somewhat flippant and careless way in which he narrated it. Whatever punishment was in store for him, I felt that he might expect no sympathy from me. Sherlock Holmes and Jones sat with their hands upon their knees, deeply interested in the story, but with the same disgust written upon their faces. He may have observed it, for there was a touch of defiance in his voice and manner as he proceeded.

"It was all very bad, no doubt," said he. "I should like to know how many fellows in my shoes would have refused a share of this

Comment [JB(]: AO1 - As narrator, Small is attempting to curry favour with his listeners, by reminding them how he is keeping his promise. Although he has

Comment [JB(]: AO3 – In keeping with the generic conventions of detective fiction, the criminal has admitted that serious crimes have taken place: murder

Comment [JB(]: AO1 - It seems as if Holmes has some sympathy for Small, or at least for his story, given that he is giving him 'whisky-and-water' to continue

Comment [JB(]: AO3 – The words 'utmost horror' make his heinous crimes fit into the genre of the gothic, in Watson's opinion, at least.

Comment [JB(]: AO2 – The use of hackneyed figurative language makes it seem as if Watson is a typical Victorian man in his reaction to Small. We, as

Comment [JB(]: AO1 – Watson is particularly disgusted by Small's seeming lack of remorse and is unimpressed by the way the latter has told the story. We can

Comment [JB(]: AO1 – Despite their professional curiosity, even Holmes and Jones are disgusted by Small's story.

Comment [JB(]: AO2 – The abstract noun 'defiance' implies a lack of remorse. If that is the case, it is very difficult for any one to sympathise with this criminal.

JOE BROADFOOT

loot when they knew that they would have their throats cut for their pains. Besides, it was my life or his when once he was in the fort. If he had got out, the whole business would come to light, and I should have been court-martialled and shot as likely as not; for people were not very lenient at a time like that."

"Go on with your story," said Holmes, shortly.

AQA-style Specimen Assessment Material 9:
Starting with this extract, explore how Conan Doyle build up an atmosphere of fear and terror in *The Sign of Four*.
Write about:
• how does Conan Doyle build up an atmosphere of fear and terror present Watson in this extract
• how does Conan Doyle build up an atmosphere of fear and terror in the novel as a whole.

EXTRACT

Sir Arthur Conan Doyle: The Sign of Four
Read the following extract from Chapter 5 of The Sign of Four and then answer the question.
In this extract, Holmes, Watson, Mary Morstan and Thaddeus Sholto have arrived at Pondicherry Lodge to see Thaddeus's brother, Batholomew. Holmes has just looked through the keyhole into Bartholomew's room and looks shocked by what he has just seen. The extract is important for it is one of the most horrific moments in the narrative.

"There is something devilish in this, Watson," said he, more moved than I had ever before seen him. "What do you make of it?"

I stooped to the hole, and recoiled in horror. Moonlight was streaming into the room, and it was bright with a vague and shifty radiance. Looking straight at me, and suspended, as it were, in the air, for all beneath was in shadow, there hung a face—the very

96

Comment [JB(]: AO2 – The use of a rhetorical question in Small's narrative makes him appear persuasive. It appears he is using his skills to try to justify the unjustifiable, which makes him appear as

Comment [JB(]: AO1 – In his matter-of-fact way, Small makes it sound as if it were his life or the merchant's. It appears that Small is not a man of honour, which makes him seem unsympathetic to the

Comment [JB(]: AO3 – The adjective 'devilish' connects with the genre of gothic horror, as it is almost as if Holmes suspects a supernatural force is at work. Being the rational person that he is,

Comment [JB(]: AO1 – The verb 'recoiled' implies that the shock of what is seen is extremely horrific. At this stage, it is fear of the unknown for the reader, as the narrator has not yet disclosed what

Comment [JB(]: AO2 – The personification of the 'moonlight' makes the night seem all the more dangerous. The fact that it is 'streaming into the room' makes it appear as if it is powerful

Comment [JB(]: AO1 – Through the setting, the writer conveys the unknown. It is difficult to pin down what exactly has happened with only the 'vague and shifty radiance' of the moonlight to operate in.

Comment [JB(]: AO2 – The words 'suspended', 'shadow' and 'hung' connote death by hanging, which to the fear and terror which have already been created in the extract.

THE SIGN OF FOUR – STUDY GUIDE

face of our companion Thaddeus. There was the same high, shining head, the same circular bristle of red hair, the same bloodless countenance. The features were set, however, in a horrible smile, a fixed and unnatural grin, which in that still and moonlit room was more jarring to the nerves than any scowl or contortion. So like was the face to that of our little friend that I looked round at him to make sure that he was indeed with us. Then I recalled to mind that he had mentioned to us that his brother and he were twins.

"This is terrible!" I said to Holmes. "What is to be done?"

"The door must come down," he answered, and, springing against it, he put all his weight upon the
lock. It creaked and groaned, but did not yield. Together we flung ourselves upon it once more, and this time it gave way with a sudden snap, and we found ourselves within Bartholomew Sholto's chamber.

> **Comment [JB():** AO3 – Bartholomew is the gothic double of his brother, Thaddeus. This also adds to the fear factor, as these identical twins give a sense of the uncanny, which links to the gothic genre.

> **Comment [JB():** AO2 – Using a triplet, the writer conveys the idea of how atrocious the dead body looks: its grin is 'horrible', 'fixed' and 'unnatural'. This adds tension heightening the horror and fear felt by the reader and the characters.

> **Comment [JB():** AO1 – Watson's reaction to the horror is ask Holmes what should done. Although Watson has been involved in a war in Afghanistan, the atrocity that has met his eyes appears to be far worse.

> **Comment [JB():** AO2 – The writer uses onomatopoeia to add drama to breaking in of the door. The noise of the 'snap' makes this appear to herald another moment of horror as they find themselves in Bartholomew's bedroom.

AQA-style Specimen Assessment Material 10:
Starting with this extract, explore the ideas conveyed about the British Empire by Conan Doyle in *The Sign of Four*.
Write about:
• how does Conan Doyle convey ideas about the British Empire in this extract
• how does Conan Doyle convey ideas about the British Empire in the novel as a whole.

EXTRACT

Sir Arthur Conan Doyle: The Sign of Four
Read the following extract from Chapter 8 of The Sign of Four and then answer the question.
In this extract, Holmes and Watson are discussing the murder of Bartholomew. Holmes is just about to look in an encyclopaedia to find out more background information on the racial identity of Jonathan Small's associate, who fired a

JOE BROADFOOT

dart from a blow pipe into Bartholomew's neck. The extract is important for it reveals the some of the prevalent attitudes of the Victorian age.

He stretched his hand up, and took down a bulky volume from the shelf. "This is the first volume
of a gazetteer which is now being published. It may be looked upon as the very latest authority.
What have we here? 'Andaman Islands, situated 340 miles to the north of Sumatra, in the Bay of
Bengal.' Hum! hum! What's all this? Moist climate, coral reefs, sharks, Port Blair, convict-barracks, Rutland Island, cottonwoods—Ah, here we are. 'The aborigines of the Andaman Islands may perhaps
claim the distinction of being the smallest race upon this earth, though some anthropologists prefer the Bushmen of Africa, the Digger Indians of America, and the Terra del Fuegians. The average height is rather below four feet, although many full-grown adults may be found who are very much smaller than this. They are a fierce, morose, and intractable people, though capable of forming most devoted friendships when their confidence has once been gained.' Mark that, Watson. Now, then, listen to this. 'They are naturally hideous, having large, misshapen heads, small, fierce eyes, and distorted features. Their feet and hands, however, are remarkably small. So intractable and fierce are they that all the efforts of the British official have failed to win them over in any degree. They have always been a terror to shipwrecked crews, braining the survivors with their stone-headed clubs, or shooting them with their poisoned arrows. These massacres are invariably concluded by a cannibal feast.' Nice, amiable people, Watson! If this fellow had been left to his own unaided devices this affair might have taken an even more ghastly turn. I fancy that, even as it is, Jonathan Small would give a good deal not to have employed him."

AQA-style Specimen Assessment Material 11:
Starting with this extract, explore how Conan Doyle presents

> **Comment [JB(]:** AO3 – The Andaman Islands were colonised by Britain and were used as a penal colony following the Indian Rebellion of 1857. The British

> **Comment [JB(]:** AO2 – The writer uses triplets to show how dangerous the people are that are native to the Andamans. Each adjective is negative

> **Comment [JB(]:** AO1 – A positive generalisation indicates that Andaman Islanders can be befriended, if approached with caution. Despite this

> **Comment [JB(]:** AO1 – The description matches the narrator's report on how Tonga looks later in the novella.
> AO3 – Many Victorians believed in the

> **Comment [JB(]:** AO1 – The word 'efforts' implies the British have tried very hard to 'win them over', but it has all been to no avail.

> **Comment [JB(]:** AO2 – The –ing form of the verbs 'braining' or 'shooting' makes it appear that these activities are still continuing.

> **Comment [JB(]:** AO1 – These horrific details paint a vivid and detailed pictures of wild and dangerous Andaman Islanders, who seem ready to eat human

> **Comment [JB(]:** AO1 – Here, Holmes uncharacteristically jumps to conclusions. It does not necessarily follow that the Andaman Islander is more vicious than

> **Comment [JB(]:** AO1 – This makes it sounds as if Jonathan Small's biggest crime is to have employed Tonga. We can only assume that partly because Small is

98

THE SIGN OF FOUR – STUDY GUIDE

the theme of greed and avarice in *The Sign of Four*.
Write about:
• how does Conan Doyle present the theme of greed and avarice in this extract
• how does Conan Doyle present the theme of greed and avarice in the novel as a whole.

EXTRACT

Sir Arthur Conan Doyle: The Sign of Four
Read the following extract from Chapter 4 of The Sign of Four and then answer the question.

In this extract, through Thaddeus's embedded narrative, we hear the last words of his father, Major John Sholto, on his death bed. The extract is important for it explores the theme of avarice, implying also that crime does not pay.

" 'I have only one thing,' he [Major John Sholto] said, 'which weighs upon my mind at this supreme moment. It is my treatment of poor Morstan's orphan [Mary]. The cursed greed which has been my besetting sin through life has withheld from her the treasure, half at least of which should have been hers. And yet I have made no use of it myself—so blind and foolish a thing is avarice. The mere feeling of possession has been so dear to me that I could not bear to share it with another. See that chaplet dipped with pearls beside the quinine-bottle. Even that I could not bear to part with, although I had got it out with the design of sending it to her. You, my sons, will give her a fair share of the Agra treasure. But send her nothing—not even the chaplet—until I am gone. After all, men have been as bad as this and have recovered.

" 'I will tell you how Morstan died,' he continued. 'He had suffered for years from a weak heart, but he concealed it from every one. I alone knew it. When in India, he and I, through a remarkable chain of circumstances, came into possession of a considerable treasure. I brought it over to England, and on the night of Morstan's arrival he came straight over here to claim his share. He walked over from the station, and was admitted by my faithful Lal Chowdar, who is now dead. Morstan and I had a

Comment [JB(): AO2 – The personification of the word 'greed' implies that this sin is so powerful that it can completely dominate someone's

Comment [JB(): AO1 – Major Sholto, at least, admits that 'half' of the treasure should belong to Mary, now that he is on his death bed. The reader may think there

Comment [JB(): AO1 – Major Sholto does not really need the extra treasure, so it is difficult to understand why greed and avarice makes him keep hold of it.

Comment [JB(): AO1 – Major Sholto admits that avarice is 'blind and foolish', personifying it again. However, he cannot seem to shake its grip.

Comment [JB(): AO1 – Major Sholto tries to explain how it feels to be consumed by greed and avarice, but it is difficult for readers to sympathise with his

Comment [JB(): AO2 – The religious imagery of the 'chaplet', which is essentially made up of prayer bead, makes the reader aware of how the

Comment [JB(): AO3 – Quinine is used to treat malaria and it reminds the reader that Major Sholto is based abroad, where illnesses of this kind are prevalent.

Comment [JB(): AO1 – Even Captain Morstan is suffering from physical ills, which seem to tie in with his mental weakness when it comes to the

JOE BROADFOOT

difference of opinion as to the division of the treasure, and we came to heated words. Morstan had sprung out of his chair in a paroxysm of anger, when he suddenly pressed his hand to his side, his face turned a dusky hue, and he fell backwards, cutting his head against the corner of the treasure-chest. When I stooped over him I found, to my horror, that he was dead.

> Comment [JB(]: AO1 – The division of the treasure causes an argument, which makes greed and avarice appear to be particularly dangerous sin.

> Comment [JB(]: AO2 – The adjective 'heated' conveys the idea that the words have become hotter as tempers are lost arguing about money.

> Comment [JB(]: AO2 – The word 'sprung' makes Captian Morstan appear to be like a wild cat. It is obvious that greed and avarice bring out the inhumane

> Comment [JB(]: AO1 – The emotional outburst shows the reader that greed and avarice can take someone over completely and make them unreasonable

> Comment [JB(]: AO1 – Interestingly, it is literally the treasure itself that causes the last injury to Captain Morstan. Metaphorically, he has been consumed

AQA-style Specimen Assessment Material 12:
Starting with this extract, explore how Conan Doyle contrasts the methods and character of Athelney Jones with Sherlock Holmes.
Write about:
• how does Conan Doyle contrast the methods and character of Athelney Jones with Sherlock Holmes in this extract
• how does Conan Doyle contrast the methods and character of Athelney Jones with Sherlock Holmes in the novel as a whole.

EXTRACT

Sir Arthur Conan Doyle: The Sign of Four
Read the following extract from Chapter 6 of The Sign of Four and then answer the question.
In this extract, Athelney Jones has just arrived to investigate the murder of Batholomew Sholto. Thaddeus's brother. Holmes is expecting the arrival of the police, as he sent Thaddeus to the police station to report the matter to them. The extract is important for it allows the reader to compare the work of the police, who had a poor reputation in the nineteenth-century, with that of Holmes.

As he [Holmes] spoke, the steps which had been coming nearer sounded loudly on the passage, and a very stout, portly man in a grey suit strode heavily into the room. He was red-faced, burly and plethoric, with a pair of very small twinkling eyes which looked keenly out from between swollen and puffy pouches. He was closely followed by an inspector in uniform, and by the still

> Comment [JB(]: AO2 – We can sense the arrival of a heavy man, judging by the 'steps' which 'sounded loudly'. The sound imagery implies that this policeman may

> Comment [JB(]: AO1 – The description of Athelney Jones refers to him being overweight and being dressed in grey. This is contrast to the impression we get

> Comment [JB(]: AO2 – The use of a triple emphasises how physically unfit Jones is. The fact that he is 'red-faced' implies that he has an unhealthy lifestyle

> Comment [JB(]: AO1 – Jones appears to look like a pig, in this description.
> AO2 – The alliteration of 'puffy pouches' emphasises how chubby and pig-like

100

THE SIGN OF FOUR – STUDY GUIDE

palpitating Thaddeus Sholto.

"Here's a business!" he cried, in a muffled, husky voice. "Here's a pretty business! But who are all these? Why, the house seems to be as full as a rabbit-warren!"

"I think you must recollect me, Mr. Athelney Jones," said Holmes, quietly.

"Why, of course I do!" he wheezed. "It's Mr. Sherlock Holmes, the theorist. Remember you! I'll never forget how you lectured us all on causes and inferences and effects in the Bishopgate jewel case. It's true you set us on the right track; but you'll own now that it was more by good luck than good guidance."

"It was a piece of very simple reasoning."

"Oh, come, now, come! Never be ashamed to own up. But what is all this? Bad business! Bad business! Stern facts here,—no room for theories. How lucky that I happened to be out at Norwood over another case! I was at the station when the message arrived. What d'you think the man died of?"

"Oh, this is hardly a case for me to theorize over," said Holmes, dryly.

"No, no. Still, we can't deny that you hit the nail on the head sometimes. Dear me! Door locked, I understand. Jewels worth half a million missing. How was the window?"

"Fastened; but there are steps on the sill."

"Well, well, if it was fastened the steps could have nothing to do with the matter. That's common sense. Man might have died in a fit; but then the jewels are missing. Ha! I have a theory. These flashes come upon me at times.—Just step outside, sergeant, and you, Mr. Sholto. Your friend can remain.— What do you think of this, Holmes? Sholto was, on his own confession, with his brother last night. The brother died in a fit, on which Sholto walked off with the treasure. How's that?"

> **Comment [JB(]:** AO2 – The use of sound imagery adds to the idea that Jones is
>
> **Comment [JB(]:** AO1 – By contrast, Holmes is 'quietly' confident that Jones
>
> **Comment [JB(]:** AO2 – Sound imagery reveals how unfit Jones is. He clearly has a
>
> **Comment [JB(]:** AO1 – Jones is quite disparaging about Holmes's methods. He
>
> **Comment [JB(]:** AO1 – Jones credits Holmes with superior knowledge and
>
> **Comment [JB(]:** AO1 – Jones puts Holmes's success down to 'good luck'
>
> **Comment [JB(]:** AO1 – Holmes believes his success in the Bishopgate jewel case
>
> **Comment [JB(]:** AO2 – Jones keeps repeating the same phrase, which is made
>
> **Comment [JB(]:** AO3 – Jones's belief in luck implies that he is not a very efficient
>
> **Comment [JB(]:** AO1 – Holmes's impatience with Jones's is apparent, as
>
> **Comment [JB(]:** AO2 – Jones uses a hackneyed phrase to grudgingly praise
>
> **Comment [JB(]:** AO1 – Jones is ready to jump to erroneous conclusions in the
>
> **Comment [JB(]:** AO1 – Jones's 'theory' is laughable. He shows how incompetent

101

JOE BROADFOOT

["On which the dead man very considerately got up and locked the door on the inside."]

AQA-style Specimen Assessment Material 13:
Starting with this extract, write about how Conan Doyle created tension.
Write about:
• how Conan Doyle presents tension in this extract
• how Conan Doyle presents tension in the novel as a whole.

EXTRACT

Sir Arthur Conan Doyle: The Sign of Four
Read the following extract from Chapter 10 of The Sign of Four and then answer the question.
In this extract, Holmes, Watson and Athelney Jones are in pursuit of the 'Aurora' on the Thames. This chase scene is just one example of how Conan Doyle produces tension and suspense in the novella, and this extract is important, as it is the climactic scene. If the pursuit is successful, Holmes and his associates will possibly be able to capture the criminals and the stolen treasure.

Our boilers were strained to their utmost, and the frail shell vibrated and creaked with the fierce energy which was driving us along. We had shot through the Pool, past the West India Docks, down the long Deptford Reach, and up again after rounding the Isle of Dogs. The dull blur in front of us resolved itself now clearly enough into the dainty *Aurora*. Jones turned our search-light upon her, so that we could plainly see the figures upon her deck. One man sat by the stern, with something black between his knees over which he stooped. Beside him lay a dark mass which looked like a Newfoundland dog. The boy held the tiller, while against the red glare of the furnace I could see old Smith, stripped to the waist, and shovelling coals for dear life. They may have had some doubt at first as to whether we were really pursuing them, but now as we

Comment [JB(]: AO3 – Holmes makes Jones look ridiculous here, which ties in with the idea that police were generally

Comment [JB(]: AO2 – The personification of the boilers being 'strained' adds to the tension in this

Comment [JB(]: AO2 – The superlative 'utmost' exaggerates how strained the boilers are, increasing the tension as the

Comment [JB(]: AO2 – The adjective 'frail' and the noun 'shell' add to the impression that the ship that Holmes is

Comment [JB(]: AO2 – The writer works through the senses to produce an almost five-dimensional effect. Here we learn

Comment [JB(]: AO3 – Like the London fog setting, elsewhere, this 'dull blur' obscures Holmes's criminals, making

Comment [JB(]: AO1 – The writer uses the idea of a 'search-light' to increase the drama, as the reader can imagine

Comment [JB(]: AO1 – The gradual revealing of exactly what is on the 'Aurora' adds tension, as sights are slowly

Comment [JB(]: AO3 – The narrative taps into the genre of realism here, as the first-person narrator describes what he

Comment [JB(]: AO2 – This colloquial turn of phrase seems apt to describe 'old Smith', as he is far from being an upper

THE SIGN OF FOUR – STUDY GUIDE

followed every winding and turning which they took there could no longer be any question about it. At Greenwich we were about three hundred paces behind them. At Blackwall we could not have been more than two hundred and fifty. I have coursed many creatures in many countries during my checkered career, but never did sport give me such a wild thrill as this mad, flying man-hunt down the Thames. Steadily we drew in upon them, yard by yard. In the silence of the night we could hear the panting and clanking of their machinery. The man in the stern still crouched upon the deck, and his arms were moving as though he were busy, while every now and then he would look up and measure with a glance the distance which still separated us. Nearer we came and nearer. Jones yelled to them to stop. We were not more than four boat's lengths behind them, both boats flying at a tremendous pace.

> Comment [JB(]: AO3 – Real place names add to the tension, as the realism created makes the action appear more plausible.
>
> Comment [JB(]: AO2 – The writer uses a countdown of 'three hundred paces' to 'two hundred and fifty' to add tension and suspense.
>
> Comment [JB(]: AO2 – The writer's use of alliteration emphasises how experienced Watson is, so if the narrator has 'never' been this thrilled before then
>
> Comment [JB(]: AO2 – the writer uses alliteration and the metaphor of 'flying' to show how the pursuit can be seen as thrilling, exciting and tense for the
>
> Comment [JB(]: AO2 – The use of sound imagery and personification heightens the tension. We can hear that the 'Aurora' is also straining itself, as we learn it is
>
> Comment [JB(]: AO1 – Despite the search-light, not everything is apparent. The narrator does not tell us the identity of the 'man in the stern' and this adds
>
> Comment [JB(]: AO2 – The writer begins to use short sentences to crank up the 'pace', which is a word used at the end of the extract.
>
> Comment [JB(]: AO2 – The writer uses the metaphor of 'flying', for a second time, to emphasise the speed of the chase and add to the tension.
>
> Comment [JB(]: AO1 – The writer literally tells us that both vessels are moving extremely quickly. This makes this chase scene appear to be more exciting.

AQA-style Specimen Assessment Material 14:
Starting with this extract, write about how Conan Doyle creates a sense of excitement in *The Sign of Four*.
Write about:
• how Conan Doyle presents excitement in this extract
• how Conan Doyle presents excitement in the novel as a whole.

EXTRACT

Sir Arthur Conan Doyle: The Sign of Four
Read the following extract from Chapter 10 of The Sign of Four and then answer the question.
In this extract, Holmes, Watson and Athelney Jones are pursuing the 'Aurora'. They aim to capture the criminals and treasure on board that vessel and have just spotted her. Holmes has noted that the 'Aurora' is 'going like the devil' and has instructed the engineer on their boat to go at full speed 'in order to catch her. The extract is important as it is swiftly nearing the climactic scene, which will involves a showdown.

103

Now she was flying down the stream, near in to the shore, going at a tremendous rate. Jones looked gravely at her and shook his head.

"She is very fast," he said. "I doubt if we shall catch her."

"We must catch her!" cried Holmes, between his teeth. "Heap it on, stokers! Make her do all she can! If we burn the boat we must have them!"

We were fairly after her now. The furnaces roared, and the powerful engines whizzed and clanked, like a great metallic heart. Her sharp, steep prow cut through the river-water and sent two rolling waves to right and to left of us. With every throb of the engines we sprang and quivered like a living thing. One great yellow lantern in our bows threw a long, flickering funnel of light in front of us. Right ahead a dark blur upon the water showed where the Aurora lay, and the swirl of white foam behind her spoke of the pace at which she was going. We flashed past barges, steamers, merchant-vessels, in and out, behind this one and round the other. Voices hailed us out of the darkness, but still the Aurora thundered on, and still we followed close upon her track.

"Pile it on, men, pile it on!" cried Holmes, looking down into the engine-room, while the fierce glow from below beat upon his eager, aquiline face.

AQA-style Specimen Assessment Material 15:
Starting with this extract, write about how Conan Doyle presents the relationship between Holmes and Watson.
Write about:
• how Conan Doyle presents their relationship in this extract
• how Conan Doyle presents their relationship in the novel as a whole.

EXTRACT

Sir Arthur Conan Doyle: The Sign of Four

Comments:
- AO2 – The use of the metaphor 'flying' emphasises to the
- AO2 – The writer uses straightforward language to re-emphasise
- AO2 – The adverb 'gravely' suggests Jones pessimism at
- AO1 – The writer shows us through Jones's action how impossible
- AO3 – Jones is at odds with Holmes, as the former is now
- AO3 – The chase is a generic convention of detective fiction.
- AO2 – After showing Jones's doubts, the writer allows the
- AO2 – The writer has Holmes's speaking in the imperative with
- AO1 – Holmes is portrayed as the most determined to
- AO1 – The narrator informs us of their progress, adding
- AO2 – A combination of personification and sound imagery adds
- AO2 – This simile reminds us that pursuers are all one in
- AO2 – The personification of the 'Aurora' makes the
- AO2 – The metaphor 'flashed' reminds us that the craft in
- AO2 – The adjective 'fierce' reminds the reader that Holmes is

THE SIGN OF FOUR – STUDY GUIDE

Read the following extract from Chapter 1 of The Sign of Four and then answer the question.
In this extract, Holmes and Watson are in conversation.

Holmes has been bragging about his 'several monographs', which are pieces of writing on a specialist subject. He claims that the differences in different types of tobacco ash are obvious to him. The extract is important as it reminds the reader how Watson is in awe of Holmes and how their discussion reveals is a teacher-pupil relationship.

"You have an extraordinary genius for minutiae," I remarked.

"I appreciate their importance. Here is my monograph upon the tracing of footsteps, with some remarks upon the uses of plaster of Paris as a preserver of impresses. Here, too, is a curious little work upon the influence of a trade upon the form of the hand, with lithotypes of the hands of slaters, sailors, corkcutters, compositors, weavers, and diamond-polishers. That is a matter of great practical interest to the scientific detective,— especially in cases of unclaimed bodies, or in discovering the antecedents of criminals. But I weary you with my hobby."

"Not at all," I answered, earnestly. "It is of the greatest interest to me, especially since I have had the opportunity of observing your practical application of it. But you spoke just now of observation and deduction. Surely the one to some extent implies the other."

"Why, hardly," he answered, leaning back luxuriously in his armchair, and sending up thick blue wreaths from his pipe. "For example, observation shows me that you have been to the Wigmore Street Post-Office this morning, but deduction lets me know that when there you dispatched a telegram."

"Right!" said I. "Right on both points! But I confess that I don't see how you arrived at it. It was a sudden impulse upon my part, and I have mentioned it to no one."

"It is simplicity itself," he remarked, chuckling at my surprise,—

105

Comment [JB(]: AO3 – Generically, detective fiction is characterised by an

Comment [JB(]: AO1 – The narrator quickly reveals how much he admires

Comment [JB(]: AO1 – Holmes clearly feels proud of his own writing

Comment [JB(]: AO2 – Holmes's gloating over his achievements is

Comment [JB(]: AO3 – The study of lithotypes or imprints gives Holmes a

Comment [JB(]: AO2 – The use of a list emphasises the number of different types

Comment [JB(]: AO1 – For the first time in this extract, Holmes shows

Comment [JB(]: AO2 – The use of the superlative 'greatest' reminds the reader

Comment [JB(]: AO1 – Holmes is quite dismissive of Watson's suggestion that

Comment [JB(]: AO2 – The use of alliteration emphasises how relaxed

Comment [JB(]: AO2 – Holmes is portrayed as producing 'wreaths' of

Comment [JB(]: AO1 – Holmes spells out the clear difference between

Comment [JB(]: AO2 – The repetition of the word 'right' shows how perfect

Comment [JB(]: AO1 – Watson confesses his ignorance, which gives

Comment [JB(]: AO3 – Another generic convention found in detective fiction

Comment [JB(]: AO1 – Holmes is quite patronising towards Watson, by

Comment [JB(]: AO2 – The sound imagery of the word 'chuckling' makes it

JOE BROADFOOT

AQA-style Specimen Assessment Material 16:
Starting with this extract, write about how Conan Doyle presents the exotic.
Write about:
• how Conan Doyle presents Tonga in this extract
• how Conan Doyle presents the exotic in the novel as a whole.

EXTRACT

Sir Arthur Conan Doyle: The Sign of Four
Read the following extract from Chapter 10 of The Sign of Four and then answer the question.
In this extract, Holmes, Watson and Athelney Jones are closing in on the 'Aurora' after chasing the vessel up the Thames. This extract is important, as it gives the reader a glimpse of the criminals. We have just viewed the man with the 'wooden stump' and now we are given a description of Tonga, who is not from England, as is therefore exotic. However, the description is far from flattering, giving us a negative view of him, while reflecting the racist attitudes and assumptions of the late Victorian era.

At the sound of his strident, angry cries there was movement in the huddled bundle upon the deck. It straightened itself into a little black man—the smallest I have ever seen—with a great, misshapen head and a shock of tangled, dishevelled hair. Holmes had already drawn his revolver, and I whipped out mine at the sight of this savage, distorted creature. He was wrapped in some sort of dark ulster or blanket, which left only his face exposed; but that face was enough to give a man a sleepless night. Never have I seen features so deeply marked with all bestiality and cruelty. His small eyes glowed and burned with a sombre light, and his thick lips were writhed back from his teeth, which grinned and chattered at us with a half animal fury.

"Fire if he raises his hand," said Holmes, quietly. We were within a boat's-length by this time, and almost within touch of our quarry. I can see the two of them now as they stood, the white man with

> Comment [JB(]: AO1 – This unflattering description of the 'little black man' makes Tonga appear physically ugly like an
>
> Comment [JB(]: AO2 – The word 'shock' subtly implies that the narrator is unpleasantly surprised by Tonga's
>
> Comment [JB(]: AO1 – The writer conveys the idea that Tonga is wild and untamed through this description of his
>
> Comment [JB(]: AO2 – The writer uses sibilance to emphasise the snake-like danger presented by Tonga.
>
> Comment [JB(]: AO1 – The writer compares Tonga's face to the stuff of nightmares, by telling the reader that his
>
> Comment [JB(]: AO2 – The use of the hyperbolic 'never' adds to the idea that the narrator has not seen anything so
>
> Comment [JB(]: AO1 – The exotic Tonga is presented here as animalistic and cruel. We have no back story for this character,
>
> Comment [JB(]: AO2 – The use of semantic field of fire subtly links Tonga with hell, making this exotic man appear
>
> Comment [JB(]: AO1 – The writer uses stereotypical racial ideas to negatively portray Tonga as different physically to
>
> Comment [JB(]: AO2 – Using triplets and personification, the writer conveys how Tonga's lips almost have a life of
>
> Comment [JB(]: AO1 – The writer does not appear to recognise Tonga as a full human being, implying that he is

THE SIGN OF FOUR – STUDY GUIDE

his legs far apart, shrieking out curses, and the unhallowed dwarf with his hideous face, and his strong yellow teeth gnashing at us in the light of our lantern.

It was well that we had so clear a view of him. Even as we looked he plucked out from under his covering a short, round piece of wood, like a school-ruler, and clapped it to his lips. Our pistols rang out together. He whirled round, threw up his arms, and with a kind of choking cough fell sideways into the stream. I caught one glimpse of his venomous, menacing eyes amid the white swirl of the waters.

> **Comment [JB(]:** AO3 – The language of the gothic, like 'unhallowed' and 'hideous', works here to portray Tonga as a creature from hell.

> **Comment [JB(]:** AO1 – The animal-like portrayal of Tonga continues as he is represented here as a ferocious, vicious beast who would like to bite his pursuers.

> **Comment [JB(]:** AO2 – The schoolboy simile makes Tonga's weaponry appear extremely basic and rudimentary.

> **Comment [JB(]:** AO1 – Even when Tonga dies, there is no sympathy in the description of the man. Clearly, Conan Doyle wants us to see Tonga as completely evil with no chance of redemption.
> AO2 – The adjective 'venomous' adds to the idea that Tonga is as dangerous as a snake with poisonous fangs.

AQA Specimen Assessment Material 17: 'Sherlock Holmes is a brilliant early example of a fictional detective.'
Starting with this extract, how far do you agree with this statement?
Write about:
• how Conan Doyle presents Holmes in this extract
• how Conan Doyle presents Holmes in the novel as a whole.

EXTRACT

Sir Arthur Conan Doyle: The Sign of Four

Read the following extract from Chapter 1 of The Sign of Four and then answer the question.
In this extract, Watson has just challenged Holmes to work out who is the owner of a watch. The detective has successfully deduced, using the balance of probability 'that it belonged to Watson's brother, much to the annoyance of the latter, who asks if it was 'guess-work'. The extract is important for it allows the reader to better understand the workings of Holmes's mind and character. Additionally, it provides us with a good explanation of deductive reasoning and how Holmes uses inference to help him solve mysteries.

JOE BROADFOOT

"No, no: I never guess. It is a shocking habit,—destructive to the logical faculty. What seems strange to you is only so because you do not follow my train of thought or observe the small facts upon which large inferences may depend. For example, I began by stating that your brother was careless. When you observe the lower part of that watch-case you notice that it is not only dinted in two places, but it is cut and marked all over from the habit of keeping other hard objects, such as coins or keys, in the same pocket. Surely it is no great feat to assume that a man who treats a fifty-guinea watch so cavalierly must be a careless man. Neither is it a very far-fetched inference that a man who inherits one article of such value is pretty well provided for in other respects."

I nodded, to show that I followed his reasoning.

"It is very customary for pawnbrokers in England, when they take a watch, to scratch the number of the ticket with a pin-point upon the inside of the case. It is more handy than a label, as there is no risk of the number being lost or transposed. There are no less than four such numbers visible to my lens on the inside of this case. Inference,—that your brother was often at low water. Secondary inference,—that he had occasional bursts of prosperity, or he could not have redeemed the pledge. Finally, I ask you to look at the inner plate, which contains the key-hole. Look at the thousands of scratches all round the hole,—marks where the key has slipped. What sober man's key could have scored those grooves? But you will never see a drunkard's watch without them. He winds it at night, and he leaves these traces of his unsteady hand. Where is the mystery in all this?"

AQA-style Specimen Assessment Material 18:
Starting with this extract, explore how Conan Doyle creates a sense of mystery.
Write about:

• how Conan Doyle uses places to create a sense of mystery in this extract

Comment [JB(]: AO2 – This emphatic statement makes Holmes appear to be extremely strange and proud of the fact that he will not lower himself to merely

Comment [JB(]: AO1 – Holmes's observation of the finer details of the watch indicate that he is a man who notices literally everything.

Comment [JB(]: AO1 – Holmes's deductions are evidence of a sharp mind at work. He plays down his achievement in correctly deducing so much from so

Comment [JB(]: AO2 – Holmes's powers of deductive reasoning drive the plot, as he has to uncover all the fact to prove his theories are true. Additionally, his

Comment [JB(]: AO1 – Holmes's deduction leads him to safely assume that Watson's brother was 'pretty well provided for'. This gives us another

Comment [JB(]: AO2 – The word 'nodded' shows that Watson is comparatively passive compared to Holmes, who is doing all of the talking.

Comment [JB(]: AO1 – Holmes's knowledge of the world is impressive, as he even knows about the practises of pawnbrokers. Given the fact that he has a

Comment [JB(]: AO2 - The sequential markers, 'secondly' and 'finally' tell the reader that Holmes is a precise man, who logically processes information. He

THE SIGN OF FOUR – STUDY GUIDE

• how Conan Doyle creates a sense of mystery in the novel as a whole.

EXTRACT

Sir Arthur Conan Doyle: The Sign of Four
Read the following extract from Chapter 3 and then answer the question.
In this extract Holmes, Watson and Mary are on their way to their first mysterious meeting. This is an important scene, in terms of plot, as the mystery may begin to unravel once the trio have arrived at their destination. Holmes mentions to Watson, the narrator, earlier in the chapter, that their 'expedition of to-night will solve' the 'difficulties' surrounding the case.

At first I had some idea as to the direction in which we were driving; but soon, what with our pace, the fog, and my own limited knowledge of London, I lost my bearings, and knew nothing, save that we seemed to be going a very long way. Sherlock Holmes was never at fault, however, and he muttered the names as the cab rattled through squares and in and out by tortuous by-streets.

"Rochester Row," said he. "Now Vincent Square. Now we come out on the Vauxhall Bridge Road. We are making for the Surrey side, apparently. Yes, I thought so. Now we are on the bridge. You can catch glimpses of the river."

We did indeed bet a fleeting view of a stretch of the Thames with the lamps shining upon the broad, silent water; but our cab dashed on, and was soon involved in a labyrinth of streets upon the other side.

"Wordsworth Road," said my companion. "Priory Road. Lark Hall Lane. Stockwell Place. Robert Street. Cold Harbor Lane. Our quest does not appear to take us to very fashionable regions."

Comment [JB(]: AO2 – Fog adds mystery, as it is nearly impossible for Holmes and Watson to see where they are going or what they are about to

Comment [JB(]: AO1 - Watson confesses he is unfamiliar with the settings he is passing on this mysterious journey. He appears to be inferior to

Comment [JB(]: AO1 – Holmes is portrayed as a superman, who can unravel this mystery. Using the hyperbole of the word 'never', the author makes the

Comment [JB(]: AO2 – Using sound imagery, the author makes the journey appear tense and, by default, more mysterious. Holmes is 'muttering' which

Comment [JB(]: AO3 – Holmes is like a London guide, so detailed is his knowledge about the city. He is portrayed here and elsewhere as an expert sleuth

Comment [JB(]: AO2 – The word 'labyrinth' means maze and this adds more twists and turns to the journey, making the mystery appear more

Comment [JB(]: AO1 - Holmes is familiar with this mysterious route, making him appear knowledgeable and more than capable of solving this mystery.

Comment [JB(]: AO1 – Holmes is familiar with places on this mysterious route, which makes him appear knowledgeable and capable of solving the

Comment [JB(]: AO3 - This authentic place name adds realism to the setting, while symbolically suggesting through the word 'cold' that it is an uninviting place to

We had, indeed, reached a questionable and forbidding neighborhood. Long lines of dull brick houses were only relieved by the coarse glare and tawdry brilliancy of public houses at the corner. Then came rows of two-storied villas each with a fronting of miniature garden, and then again interminable lines of new staring brick buildings,—the monster tentacles which the giant city was throwing out into the country. At last the cab drew up at the third house in a new terrace. None of the other houses were inhabited, and that at which we stopped was as dark as its neighbors, save for a single glimmer in the kitchen window.

> Comment [JB(]: AO3 – The 'coarse' (which means rough) and 'tawdry' (which means cheap and tasteless) setting implies threat and danger, adding to tension surrounding the mystery. AO2 - The word 'glare' makes the personified public houses appear to be angry, as it portrays them as staring in threatening manner.

> Comment [JB(]: AO2 – The use of personification adds to the mystery, as the city appears to have as many arms as an octopus or some other sea creature. The suburban setting is not free of the grasp and possibly the inherent evil of London.

> Comment [JB(]: AO3 - The darkness of this setting makes it fall into the genre of the gothic.

AQA-style Specimen Assessment Material 19:
Starting with this extract, explore how Conan Doyle presents Holmes as an interesting and unusual investigator.
Write about:
• how Conan Doyle presents Holmes as an interesting and unusual investigator in this extract
• how Conan Doyle presents Holmes as an interesting and unusual investigator in the novel as a whole.

EXTRACT

Sir Arthur Conan Doyle: The Sign of Four
Read the following extract from Chapter 6 of The Sign of Four and then answer the question.
In this extract, Holmes is investigating the death of Bartholomew Sholto at Pondicherry Lodge. Holmes has already deduced that one of the assassins was a man with a wooden leg and now he is discussing the child-sized prints of a naked foot 'at the scene of the crime with Watson. The extract is important for it allows the reader to gain insight into Holmes's character and to see how he operates as an expert detective.

"My dear Watson, try a little analysis yourself," said he, with a touch of impatience. "You know my methods. Apply them, and it will be instructive to compare results."

> Comment [JB(]: AO1 – Holmes is instructive like a teacher to his pupil, Watson. He is an unusual investigator in that he is willing to share his deductive reasoning with Watson.

> Comment [JB(]: AO3 – Holmes is presented as an expert investigator, which fits into the genre of detective fiction. He is always honing his skills, judging by his willingness 'to compare results' with Watson.

THE SIGN OF FOUR – STUDY GUIDE

"I cannot conceive anything which will cover the facts," I answered.

"It will be clear enough to you soon," he said, in an off-hand way. "I think that there is nothing else of importance here, but I will look." He whipped out his lens and a tape measure, and hurried about the room on his knees, measuring, comparing, examining, with his long thin nose only a few inches from the planks, and his beady eyes gleaming and deep-set like those of a bird. So swift, silent, and furtive were his movements, like those of a trained blood-hound picking out a scent, that I could not but think what a terrible criminal he would have made had he turned his energy and sagacity against the law, instead of exerting them in its defense. As he hunted about, he kept muttering to himself, and finally he broke out into a loud crow of delight.

"We are certainly in luck," said he. "We ought to have very little trouble now. Number One has had the misfortune to tread in the creosote. You can see the outline of the edge of his small foot here at the side of this evil-smelling mess. The carboy has been cracked, you see, and the stuff has leaked out."

AQA-style Specimen Assessment Material 20:
Starting with this extract, write about how Conan Doyle presents Mary Morstan.
Write about:
• how Conan Doyle presents Mary Morstan in this extract
• how Conan Doyle presents Mary Morstan in the novel as a whole.

EXTRACT

Sir Arthur Conan Doyle: The Sign of Four
Read the following extract from Chapter 2 of The Sign of Four and then answer the question.
In this extract, Holmes and Watson are awaiting the arrival of Miss Mary Morstan. They have already been informed of her

---

Comment [JB(): AO1 – This equipment shows how well prepared Holmes is. It is

Comment [JB(): AO2 – It is almost as if Holmes worships his job of solving crimes,

Comment [JB(): AO2 – Ascending tricolon is used here to show the details

Comment [JB(): AO1 – This shows how keen Holmes is to solves the crime. He is

Comment [JB(): AO2 – Bird imagery makes Holmes appear to be intelligent

Comment [JB(): AO2 – This triplet emphasises how formidable Holmes's

Comment [JB(): AO2 – Blood-hound imagery makes Holmes appear to be a

Comment [JB(): AO1 – The narrator makes it clear that he feels the world is

Comment [JB(): AO1 – This portrays Holmes as eccentric and enthusiastic. He

Comment [JB(): AO2 – Sound imagery links Holmes to birds again. Crows are

Comment [JB(): AO1 – Although the reader can sense that Holmes makes his

Comment [JB(): AO3 – There is a hint of the gothic in this mention of the word

Comment [JB(): AO3 – Holmes's knowledge of the world is unparalleled.

JOE BROADFOOT

name by their landlady, Mrs Hudson, who describes her as 'a young lady'. The extract is important for it allows the reader to get a chance to form an opinion of this female character, whose mystery will drive the plot forward.

Miss Morstan entered the room with a firm step and an outward composure of manner. She was a blonde young lady, small, dainty, well gloved, and dressed in the most perfect taste. There was, however, a plainness and simplicity about her costume which bore with it a suggestion of limited means. The dress was a sombre grayish beige, untrimmed and unbraided, and she wore a small turban of the same dull hue, relieved only by a suspicion of white feather in the side. Her face had neither regularity of feature nor beauty of complexion, but her expression was sweet and amiable, and her large blue eyes were singularly spiritual and sympathetic. In an experience of women which extends over many nations and three separate continents, I have never looked upon a face which gave a clearer promise of a refined and sensitive nature. I could not but observe that as she took the seat which Sherlock Holmes placed for her, her lip trembled, her hand quivered, and she showed every sign of intense inward agitation.

"I have come to you, Mr. Holmes," she said, "because you once enabled my employer, Mrs. Cecil Forrester, to unravel a little domestic complication. She was much impressed by your kindness and skill."

"Mrs. Cecil Forrester," he repeated thoughtfully. "I believe that I was of some slight service to her. The case, however, as I remember it, was a very simple one."

"She did not think so. But at least you cannot say the same of mine. I can hardly imagine anything more strange, more utterly inexplicable, than the situation in which I find myself."

Comment [JB(]: AO1 – Mary's strength of purpose is apparent from the

Comment [JB(]: AO2 – A succession of adjectives detail Mary's feminine

Comment [JB(]: AO2 – A superlative is used here and indicates exaggeration on

Comment [JB(]: AO1 – These adjectives indicate that Mary is modest and restrains

Comment [JB(]: AO1 – The narrator has quickly decided that Mary may be

Comment [JB(]: AO2 – Negative adjectives add to the idea that something

Comment [JB(]: AO3 – The 'turban' is exotic head wear that links Mary to the

Comment [JB(]: AO1 – The writer appears to be setting Mary up as a love

Comment [JB(]: AO2 – The writer uses the sibilance of the words 'spiritual and

Comment [JB(]: AO3 – Mary is being portrayed as the ideal Victorian woman,

Comment [JB(]: AO2 – The writer uses a triplet to emphasise how feminine Mary

Comment [JB(]: AO3 – She is portrayed as a damsel in distress, which allows the

Comment [JB(]: AO3 – Victorian women are usually associated with the home.

Comment [JB(]: AO2 – Her need for help is a catalyst for the narrative.

14 ESSAY-WRITING TIPS

Essay writing tips

<u>Use a variety of connectives</u>

Have a look of this list of connectives. Which of these would you choose to use?

'ADDING' DISCOURSE MARKERS

- AND

- ALSO
- AS WELL AS
- MOREOVER
- TOO
- FURTHERMORE
- ADDITIONALLY

I hope you chose 'additionally', 'furthermore' and 'moreover'. Don't be afraid to use the lesser discourse markers, as they are also useful. Just avoid using those ones over and over again. I've seen essays from Key Stage 4 students that use the same discourse marker for the opening sentence of each paragraph! Needless to say, those essays didn't get great marks!

Okay, here are some more connectives for you to look at. Select the best ones.

'SEQUENCING' DISCOURSE MARKERS

- NEXT
- FIRSTLY
- SECONDLY
- THIRDLY
- FINALLY

- MEANWHILE
- AFTER
- THEN
- SUBSEQUENTLY

This time, I hope you chose 'subsequently' and 'meanwhile'.

Here are some more connectives for you to 'grade'!

'ILLUSTRATING / EXEMPLIFYING' DISCOURSE MARKERS

- FOR EXAMPLE
- SUCH AS
- FOR INSTANCE
- IN THE CASE OF
- AS REVEALED BY
- ILLUSTRATED BY

I'd probably go for 'illustrated by' or even 'as exemplified by' (which is not in the list!). Please feel free to add your own examples to the lists. Strong connectives impress examiners. Don't forget it! That's why I want you to look at some more.

'CAUSE & EFFECT' DISCOURSE MARKERS

- BECAUSE
- SO
- THEREFORE
- THUS
- CONSEQUENTLY
- HENCE

I'm going for 'consequently' this time. How about you? What about the next batch?

'COMPARING' DISCOURSE MARKERS

- SIMILARLY
- LIKEWISE
- AS WITH
- LIKE
- EQUALLY
- IN THE SAME WAY

I'd choose 'similarly' this time. Still some more to go.

'QUALIFYING' DISCOURSE MARKERS

- BUT
- HOWEVER

- WHILE
- ALTHOUGH
- UNLESS
- EXCEPT
- APART FROM
- AS LONG AS

It's 'however' for me!

'CONTRASTING' DISCOURSE MARKERS

- WHEREAS
- INSTEAD OF
- ALTERNATIVELY
- OTHERWISE
- UNLIKE
- ON THE OTHER HAND
- CONVERSELY

I'll take 'conversely' or 'alternatively' this time.

'EMPHASISING' DISCOURSE MARKERS

- ABOVE ALL

- IN PARTICULAR

- ESPECIALLY

- SIGNIFICANTLY

- INDEED

- NOTABLY

You can breathe a sigh of relief now! It's over! No more connectives. However, now I want to put our new found skills to use in our essays.

15 LITERATURE GLOSSARY

Allegory: extended metaphor, like the grim reaper representing death, e.g. Scrooge symbolizing capitalism.

Alliteration: same consonant sound repeating, e.g. 'She sells sea shells'.

Allusion: reference to another text/person/place/event.

Ascending tricolon: sentence with three parts, each increasing in power, e.g. 'ringing, drumming, shouting'.

Aside: character speaking so some characters cannot hear what is being said. Sometimes, an aside is directly to the audience. It's a dramatic technique which reveals the character's inner thoughts and feelings.

Assonance: same vowel sounds repeating, e.g. 'Oh no, won't Joe go?'

Ballad: a poem, usually associated with love, that tells a story.

Bathos: abrupt change from sublime to ridiculous for humorous effect.

Blank verse: lines of unrhymed iambic pentameter.

Caesura: punctuation in a line of poetry that occurs before the end.

Colloquial: everyday, informal language.

Compressed time: when the narrative is fast-forwarding through the action.

Descending tricolon: sentence with three parts, each decreasing in power, e.g. 'shouting, talking, whispering'.

Denouement: tying up loose ends, the resolution.

Diction: choice of words or vocabulary.

Didactic: used to describe literature designed to inform, instruct or pass on a moral message.

Dilated time: opposite compressed time, here the narrative is in slow motion.

Direct address: second person narrative, predominantly using the personal pronoun 'you'.

Dramatic action verb: manifests itself in physical action, e.g. I punched him in the face.

Dramatic irony: audience knows something that the character is unaware of.

Dramatic monologue: when a poet adopts a different persona to address an implied listener.

Ellipsis: leaving out part of the story and allowing the reader to fill in the narrative gap.

End-stopped lines: poetic lines that end with punctuation.

Enjambment: run-over lines without punctuation at the end of a line of poetry.

Epistolary: letter or correspondence-driven narrative.

Euphemism: substituting an emotionally-charged word for something less upsetting, e.g. 'passed away' instead of 'died'.

Flashback/Analepsis: going back in time to the past, interrupting the chronological sequence.

Flashforward/Prolepsis: going forward in time to the future, interrupting the chronological sequence.

Form: type of poem e.g. sonnet or ballad etc.

Foreshadowing/Adumbrating: suggestion of plot developments that will occur later in the narrative.

Free verse: poetry without rhyme or regular rhythm.

Gothic: another strand of Romanticism, typically with a wild setting, a sensitive heroine, an older man with a 'piercing gaze', discontinuous structure, doppelgangers, guilt and the 'unspeakable' (according to Eve Kosofsky Sedgwick).

Half-rhyme/slant rhyme: words that nearly rhyme eg 'years' and 'yours'.

Hamartia: character flaw, leading to that character's downfall.

Hyperbole: exaggeration for effect.

Iambic pentameter: a line of ten syllables beginning with a lighter stress alternating with a heavier stress in its perfect form, which sounds like a heartbeat. The stress falls on the even syllables, numbers: 2, 4, 6, 8 and 10, e.g. 'When now I think you can behold such sights'.

Iambic tetrameter: a line of eight syllables beginning with a lighter stress alternating with a heavier stress in its perfect form, which sounds like a heartbeat. The stress falls on the even syllables, numbers: 2, 4, 6 and 8 e.g. 'I went across the road for tea'.

Internal rhyme: rhyming words that occur inside a single line or lines.

Intertextuality: links to other literary texts.

Irony: amusing or cruel reversal of expected outcome or words meaning the opposite to their literal meaning.

Metaphor: describing something as if it were something else e.g. 'that boy is lightning'.

Metafiction/Romantic irony: self-conscious exposure of the devices used to create 'the truth' within a work of fiction.

Metre: stressed and unstressed pattern in a poem.

Motif: recurring image use of language or idea that connects the narrative together and creates a theme or mood, e.g. 'green light' in *The Great Gatsby.*

Oxymoron: contradictory terms combined, e.g. deafening silence.

Pastiche: imitation of another's work.

Pathetic fallacy: a form of personification whereby inanimate objects show human attributes, e.g. 'the sea smiled benignly'. The originator of the term, John Ruskin in 1856, used 'the cruel, crawling foam', from Kingsley's *The Sands of Dee*, as an example to clarify what he meant by the 'morbid' nature of pathetic fallacy. Nowadays, it is often used to describe how the weather affects how the writer portrays a character's mood.

Personification: concrete or abstract object made human, often simply achieved by using a capital letter or a personal pronoun, e.g. 'Nature', or describing a ship as 'she'.

Petrarchan sonnet: the first eight lines (octave) have a regular ABBA rhyme scheme, while the last six lines (sestet) have a different rhyme scheme.

Plosive: letters that force the speaker to expel air explosively while speaking e.g. b, d, g, k, p or t.

Pun/Double entendre: a word with a double meaning, usually employed in witty wordplay but not always.

Quatrain: a four-line stanza.

Retrospective: account of events after they have occurred.

Romanticism: genre celebrating the power of imagination, spriritualism and nature.

Semantic/lexical field: related words about a single concept, e.g. king, queen and prince are all concerned with royalty.

Shakespearean sonnet: the first three quatrains have a

regular ABAB, CDCD, EFEF rhyme scheme, before ending with a GG rhyming couplet.

Soliloquy: character thinks aloud, but is not heard by other characters (unlike in a monologue) giving the audience access to inner thoughts and feelings.

Stanza/verse: a group of lines in a poem.

Structure: the order of ideas and events.

Style: choice of language, form and structure, and effects produced.

Synecdoche: one part of something referring to the whole, e.g. Carker's teeth represent him in *Dombey and Son*.

Syntax: the way words and sentences are placed together.

Tetracolon climax: sentence with four parts, culminating with the last part, e.g. 'I have nothing to offer but blood, toil, tears, and sweat ' (Winston Churchill).

Volta/turn: where the poem's tone/mood changes dramatically.

ABOUT THE AUTHOR

Joe Broadfoot is a secondary school head of English and a soccer journalist, who also writes fiction and literary criticism. His former experiences as a DJ took him to far-flung places such as Tokyo, Kobe, Beijing, Hong Kong, Jakarta, Cairo, Dubai, Cannes, Oslo, Bergen and Bodo. He is now PGCE and CELTA-qualified with QTS, a first-class honours degree in Literature and an MA in Victorian Studies (majoring in Charles Dickens). Drama is close to his heart as he acted in 'Macbeth' and 'A Midsummer Night's Dream' at the Royal Northern College of Music in Manchester.

Printed in Poland
by Amazon Fulfillment
Poland Sp. z o.o., Wrocław